THE LITTLE BOOK

OF

MARKET WIZARDS

Little Book Big Profits Series

In the *Little Book Big Profits* series, the brightest icons in the financial world write on topics that range from tried-and-true investment strategies to tomorrow's new trends. Each book offers a unique perspective on investing, allowing the reader to pick and choose from the very best in investment advice today.

Books in the *Little Book Big Profits* series include:

THE LITTLE BOOK

OF
MARKET WIZARDS

Lessons from
the Greatest Traders

JACK D. SCHWAGER

WILEY

Cover design: Paul McCarthy

Published by John Wiley & Sons, Inc., Hoboken, New Jersey.
Published simultaneously in Canada.

For general information on our other products and services or for technical support, please contact our Customer Care Department within the United States at (800) 762-2974, outside the United States at (317) 572-3993 or fax (317) 572-4002.

Wiley publishes in a variety of print and electronic formats and by print-on-demand. Some material included with standard print versions of this book may not be included in e-books or in print-on-demand. If this book refers to media such as a CD or DVD that is not included in the version you purchased, you may download this material at http://booksupport.wiley.com. For more information about Wiley products, visit www.wiley.com.

Library in Congress Cataloging-in-Publication Data:

Schwager, Jack D., 1948–
    The little book of market wizards : lessons from the greatest traders / Jack D. Schwager.
      pages   cm. — (Little books big profits series)
    ISBN 978-1-118-85869-1 (hardback) — ISBN 978-1-118-85862-2 (ePDF) — ISBN 978-1-118-85864-6 (ePub) 1. Investments. 2. Investment analysis.
    I. Title.
  HG4521.S35782547 2014
  332.6—dc23

                               2013045083

Printed in the United States of America

10 9 8 7 6 5 4 3 2 1

To Jo Ann
The most important person in my life
With love

Contents

Foreword

As a long-standing tradition each year during the Christmas to New Year's break, I watch *The Bourne Trilogy* and read Jack Schwager's *Market Wizards* series—*The Bourne Trilogy* for pure entertainment, the *Market Wizards* series to prepare me emotionally and mentally for the coming year of market combat.

No author—living or deceased—has created such a rich archive of printed material on the profession of market speculation as has Jack Schwager. An entire generation of traders owes a debt to the *Market Wizards* series and to Jack for at least some portion of its success. There is no doubt in my mind that the *Market Wizards* series will remain just as timely 80 years from now as Edwin Lefèvre's *Reminiscences of a Stock Operator* remains today.

What novice and aspiring market participant would not want to spend time with and pick the brains of 59 of the world's most successful and accomplished market traders? That is exactly what Jack Schwager's *Market Wizards* books offer, bringing to us all the insights, processes of market operations, risk management principles, and key lessons from "Hall of Fame" stock, interest rate, foreign exchange, and futures market speculators.

As someone who has lived off trading profits since 1981, I am not a fan of the how-to trading books that provide the step-by-step details of another trader's "secret sauce." I am a staunch believer that all consistently profitable traders have two things in common: an approach to the markets reflecting one's unique personality and aggressive risk management. At each reading of the *Market Wizards* books, these two components of profitable trading emerge in fresh new ways, challenging me to reflect on my own method of market speculation—past, present, and future.

The Little Book of Market Wizards brings new life to the *Market Wizards* series. In one sense, it is a CliffsNotes version—a quick reminder of all the interviews that have come before. Yet, in a different sense, the book brings remarkably new dimensions that only Jack Schwager could tease out of his extensive interviews with the trading greats.

The Little Book of Market Wizards is the thematic interpretation of Jack's five dozen interviews over four books in which he boils down all the *Market Wizards* content into buckets or categories vital for trading success.

In addition to the themes of aggressive risk management and the need for a unique personalized trading approach, which I have already mentioned, *The Little Book of Market Wizards* identifies many other common denominators shared by successful traders, with extremely useful real-life examples for each. These themes range from patience to a need for an edge, from hard work to discipline, from losing as part of the game to dealing with emotions, and from handling losing streaks to making mistakes.

Most novice and aspiring traders errantly believe that the secret to profitable trading resides in identifying trade entry signals. Clever marketers, most of whom are not successful traders, feed this false belief, offering trading systems with a 70 percent to 80 percent win rate.

All market participants—newbies or veterans, those struggling to succeed or those with a long history of profitability, discretionary or systematic traders, and private speculators or hedge fund managers—will soon add *The Little Book of Market Wizards* to their list of favorite books on trading and the markets.

With *The Little Book of Market Wizards* I have found a new book to read at the end of each year. In fact, it will be the first book I will read, reread, and read again. Thank you, Jack, for another great gift to market participants.

—Peter L. Brandt, trader

Preface

⁓

OVER THE COURSE OF the past 25 years, I have interviewed some of the world's best traders in a quest to discover what made them so successful—a project chronicled in four *Market Wizards* books. I sought to answer the question: What differentiates these traders from ordinary market participants? What common traits do they share that might explain their extraordinary success?

The Little Book of Market Wizards is a distillation of the answers to these questions. Essentially, this book provides an overview of some of the major insights garnered across the four *Market Wizards* books, spanning a quarter century. *The Little Book of Market Wizards* is not intended as a replacement for the books in the *Market Wizard* series, but rather as a pithy introduction. I have extracted the lessons that I thought were most important in the interviews conducted for the *Market Wizards* series. Individual readers, however, are likely to draw their own points of emphasis. This realization has become clear to me over the years when different readers continually mentioned different interviews as their personal favorites. Those who want to go deeper can, of course, follow up with the original interviews in the four *Market Wizards* books.

Readers with an interest in trading and investing who have not read the *Market Wizards* books should find this book provides a concentration of valuable trading advice in a concise and accessible format. Former readers of the *Market Wizards* series, however, should still find this volume useful as a convenient, concise review of the critical trading lessons embedded in the original interviews.

This book is not intended as a how-to on trading, nor is it a book on techniques for making trades. There are no suggestions or recommendations for making a fortune in the markets. Too many aspiring traders look for how-to books for a task that does not lend itself to such a formulaic treatment, while entirely missing the point that there are concepts that are essential to success in trading regardless of the methodology. Readers looking for the secret formula to making easy money in the markets will not find the answer here and are likely to be disappointed—although I would argue that they would likely be disappointed as well with the results of following the prescriptions of books that promise such an outcome. Readers who, instead, seek to build the foundation for potential success in the markets should find the ideas in *The Little Book of Market Wizards* valuable, if not essential.

Although, ostensibly, this book is about success in trading, in a broader sense, it is about success in general. Readers will find that most of the traits highlighted are equally applicable to success in any endeavor. I recall many years ago, after finishing a talk on the topic of success in trading, I was approached by one of the attendees. He introduced himself and said, "I am a minister, and I was fascinated by how many of the points you made were also critical to my success in building a congregation." Now, it is hard to get further from trading than the ministry, yet the same key elements seemed to apply. I suspect there are some common principles of success, and I have simply discovered them through the perspective of great traders.

Chapter One

Failure Is Not Predictive

The Story of Bob Gibson

On April 15, 1959, Bob Gibson played in his first major league game, coming in as a relief pitcher for the Cardinals as they trailed the Dodgers 3–0. Gibson gave up a home run to the very first batter he faced—an ignominy suffered by only 65 pitchers in the history of the game.[1] In the next inning, Gibson gave up another home run. Gibson got a chance to redeem himself coming in as a relief pitcher the next evening, but again was hit hard by the Dodgers. Two nights later, Gibson was brought in against the Giants with two outs and two runners on in the eighth inning and promptly gave up a double. After that game, Gibson sat on the bench for a week, and then was sent back to the minors. It is hard to imagine a more demoralizing beginning.

Despite his dismal start, Gibson ultimately went on to become one of the best pitchers in baseball history. He is widely considered among the top 20 pitchers of all time. Gibson played 17 seasons in the majors, winning 251 games, with 3,117 strikeouts and a 2.91 earned run average (ERA). In 1968, he posted an unbelievably low 1.12 ERA—the lowest such figure since 1914. He won two Cy Young awards, twice was named as the World Series most valuable player (MVP), played on nine All-Star teams, and was elected to the Baseball Hall of Fame in his first year of eligibility.

If at First You Fail

One of the surprises I found in doing the *Market Wizards* books was how many of these spectacularly successful traders started with failure. Stories of wipeouts, or even multiple wipeouts, were not uncommon. Michael Marcus provided a classic example.

Michael Marcus was enticed into trading futures when he was a junior in college. There he met John, a friend of a friend, who dangled the prospect of being able to double his money in two weeks by trading commodities. Marcus fell for the pitch, hired John as a trading adviser for $30 a week, and opened a futures account with the money he had scraped together in savings.

Standing in the customer gallery of the brokerage firm, watching the clicking prices on the wall-size commodity board (this was back in the 1960s), Marcus quickly realized that his "adviser," John, was clueless about trading. Marcus lost money on every trade. Then John came up with the idea that was "going to save the day." The trade was buying August pork bellies and selling February pork bellies of the following year because the price spread between the two contracts was greater than the carrying charges (the total cost of taking delivery in the nearby contract, storing the commodity, and redelivering it in the forward contract). It seemed like a can't-lose trade. After placing the trade, Marcus and John went to lunch. When they returned, Marcus was shocked to find that his account had been almost completely wiped out. (Marcus would later discover that August pork bellies were not deliverable against the February contract.) At that point, Marcus told John that he thought he knew as much as he did—which was nothing—and fired his adviser.

Marcus then managed to rustle up another $500, which he lost as well. Unwilling to give up and accept failure, Marcus decided to cash in $3,000 from the life insurance left to him by his father, who had died when he was 15. He then started reading up on grains and making some winning trades. In 1970, he bought corn based on a recommendation in a newsletter he subscribed to. By sheer luck, 1970 was the year of the corn blight. By the end of that summer, Marcus had turned the $3,000 into $30,000.

In the fall, Marcus started graduate school, but found himself so preoccupied by trading that he dropped out. He moved to New York, and when asked what he did for a living, he told people rather pompously that he was a "speculator."

In the spring of 1971, there was a theory around that the blight had wintered over and would infect the corn crop again. Marcus believed this theory as well, and he intended to capitalize on it. He borrowed $20,000 from his mother, adding it to his $30,000 account. He then used the entire $50,000 to buy the maximum number of corn and wheat contracts he could on margin. For a while, the market held steady because of the blight fears, but it didn't go higher. Then one morning, there was a financial headline that read, "More Blight on the Floor of the Chicago Board of Trade Than in Midwest Cornfields." The corn market opened sharply lower and fairly quickly moved to and locked *limit down*.[2] Marcus stood by paralyzed, hoping the market would rebound, and watching it stay locked limit down. Given that his position had been heavily margined, he had no choice but to liquidate everything the next morning. By the time he was out, he had lost his entire $30,000 plus $12,000 of the $20,000 his mother had lent him.

---- ∽ ----

**I would look up and say, "Am I really that stupid?"
And I seemed to hear a clear answer saying,
"No, you are not stupid. You just have to
keep at it." So I did.**

Michael Marcus

I asked Marcus whether with all these failures he ever thought of just giving up. Marcus replied, "I would some-times think that maybe I ought to stop trading because it was very painful to keep losing. In *Fiddler on the Roof*, there is a scene where the lead looks up and talks to God. I would look up and say, 'Am I really that stupid?' And I seemed to hear a clear answer saying, 'No, you are not stupid. You just have to keep at it.' So I did."

He did, indeed. Eventually, it all clicked for Marcus. He had an amazing innate talent as a trader. Once he com-bined this inner skill with experience and risk manage-ment, he was astoundingly successful. He took a trading job at Commodities Corporation. The firm initially funded his account with $30,000, and several years later added another $100,000. In about 10 years' time, Marcus turned those modest allocations into $80,000,000! And that was with the firm withdrawing as much as 30 percent of his profits in many years to pay the company's burgeoning expenses.

"One-Lot" Persists

Although many of the Market Wizards started off with some degree of failure, perhaps none reached the depth of despondency over their losses as did Tony Saliba. At the start of his career when he was a clerk on the floor, one of the traders staked him with $50,000. Saliba went long volatility spreads (option positions that gain if the market volatility increases). In the first two weeks, Saliba ran the account up to $75,000. He thought he was a genius. What he didn't realize was that he was buying these options at very high premiums because his purchases followed a highly volatile period. The market then went sideways and the market volatility and option premiums collapsed. In six weeks Saliba had run the account down to only $15,000.

Recounting this episode, Saliba said, "I was feeling suicidal. Do you remember the big DC-10 crash at O'Hare in May 1979, when all those people died? That was when I hit bottom."

"Was that a metaphor for your mood?" I asked.

"Yes," answered Saliba. "I would have exchanged places with one of those people in that plane on that day. I felt that bad. I thought, 'This is it; I've ruined my life.' . . . I felt like a failure."

Notwithstanding this dismal start, Saliba had one important thing going for him: persistence. After his disastrous beginning, he came close to quitting the world of trading, but ultimately decided to keep trying. He sought the advice of more experienced brokers. They taught Saliba the importance of discipline, doing homework, and a goal of consistent, moderate profitability, rather than trying to get rich quick. Saliba took these lessons to heart and switched from trading options in Teledyne, which was extremely volatile, to trading options in Boeing, which was a narrow-range market. When he did go back to trading Teledyne, his standard conservative order size led to ridicule by the other brokers and the sobriquet "One-Lot." Once again, Saliba persisted, this time putting up with all the ribbing and not being goaded into departing from his cautious approach. Ultimately, the persistence and attention to risk control paid off. At one point, Saliba put together a streak of 70 consecutive months with profits in excess of $100,000.

Two Key Lessons

There are two key lessons that can be drawn from this chapter.

First, failure is not predictive. Even great traders often encounter failure—and even repeated failures—early in their careers. Failure at the start is the norm, even for those who ultimately become Market Wizards. As a related comment, the fact that most people who attempt trading fail at the beginning suggests that all novice traders should start with small amounts of cash because they might as well pay less for their market education.

Second, persistence is instrumental to success. Most people faced with the types of failures encountered by the traders detailed in this chapter would have given up and tried some other endeavor. It would have been easy for the traders in this chapter to have done the same. Were it not for their relentless persistence, many of the Market Wizards would never have discovered their ultimate potential.

Chapter Two

What Is
Not Important

BEFORE CONSIDERING WHAT IS important to trading success, let's start with what's *not* important, because what many novice traders believe is essential to trading success is actually a diversion. Many would-be traders believe that trading success is all about finding some secret formula or system that explains and predicts price moves, and that if only they could uncover this solution to market price behavior, success would be assured. The idea that trading success is tied to finding some specific ideal approach is misguided. There is no single correct methodology.

Let me illustrate this point by comparing the trading philosophies and trading approaches of two of the traders I interviewed: Jim Rogers and Marty Schwartz.

Jim Rogers

Jim Rogers is a phenomenally successful trader, although he would insist on calling himself an investor, as opposed to trader, because of the long-term nature of his market positions. In 1973, he partnered with George Soros to start the Quantum Fund, one of the most successful hedge funds of all time. Rogers left Quantum in 1980 because the firm's success had led to expansion and with it unwanted management responsibilities. Rogers just wanted to focus on market research and investment, so he "retired" to manage his own money.

Rogers is particularly skilled in seeing the big picture and anticipating major long-term trends. When I interviewed him in 1988, gold had been declining for eight years, but Rogers seemed certain the bear market would carry on for another decade.

"Generals always fight the last war," he said. "Portfolio managers always invest in the last bull market. The idea that gold has always been a great store of value is absurd. There have been times in history when gold has lost purchasing power—sometimes for decades."

Rogers was absolutely right, as gold continued to slide for another 11 years. Another market he was particularly opinionated about was the Japanese stock market. At the time, Japanese equities were in the midst of an explosive bull market. Yet Rogers was convinced there would be a tremendous move in the opposite direction.

"I guarantee that the Japanese stock market is going to have a major collapse—possibly within the next year or two. . . . [Japanese stocks] are going to go down 80 to 90 percent."

This forecast seemed preposterous, yet it was absolutely correct. A little over a year after our conversation, the Japanese stock market peaked, beginning a slide that would see the Nikkei index lose about 80 percent of its value over the next 14 years.

Clearly, Jim Rogers is a man whose opinion is worth paying attention to. Rogers is a fundamental analyst. I asked Rogers what he thought of chart reading. His response left little question about his derisive attitude toward technical analysis.

"I haven't met a rich technician," Rogers said, "excluding, of course, technicians who sell their technical services and make a lot of money."

I then asked Rogers if he ever used charts.

"I use them," he said, "to see what is going on. . . . I don't say—what is that term you used earlier, *reversal?*—'There is a reversal here.' I don't even know what a reversal is."

When I tried to explain the term, he cut me off.

"Don't tell me. It might mess up my mind. I don't know about those things, and I don't want to know."

I doubt that it would be possible to get any more cynical about a particular trading methodology than Jim Rogers's attitude toward technical analysis.

Marty Schwartz

Now let's consider another incredibly successful trader, Marty Schwartz, who is at the other end of the spectrum in terms of analytical approach. When I interviewed Schwartz, he had run a $40,000 account into over $20 million while never realizing a drawdown of more than 3 percent (based on month-end data) in the process. Schwartz took pains to point out that his two worst months—losses of 3 percent and 2 percent—were the months his children were born and he was unavoidably distracted. During this period, he had entered 10 public trading contests. Nine of these were four-month contests in which he averaged a 210 percent return nonannualized! In his single one-year contest, he scored a 781 percent return.

Clearly, Schwartz is another trader whose opinion should be taken very seriously. What does he have to say on the topic of the efficacy of fundamental analysis versus technical analysis? He had been a securities analyst for nearly a decade before he became a full-time trader using technical analysis. When I asked Schwartz whether he had made a full transition from fundamental analysis to technical analysis, ironically, his reply seemed to be a direct retort to Rogers's comment on technical analysis—a statement I hadn't mentioned to him.

Schwartz answered, "Absolutely. I always laugh at people who say, 'I've never met a rich technician.' I love that! It is such an arrogant, nonsensical response. I used fundamentals for nine years and got rich as a technician."

It would be difficult to find two more divergent or strongly held viewpoints on what works and what doesn't work in trading the markets. Rogers has based his trading decisions solely on fundamental analysis and considers technical analysis to be on the same plane as snake oil, while Schwartz consistently lost money using fundamental analysis, but has achieved incredible performance using technical analysis. Both men have succeeded spectacularly, and both view each other's methods with complete disdain and even cynicism.

Reconciling the Divergent Views

What does the dichotomy between Rogers and Schwartz tell you? It should tell you that there is no single true path in the markets. There is no single market secret to discover, no single correct way to trade the markets. Those seeking the one true answer to the markets haven't even gotten as far as asking the right question, let alone getting the right answer.

There is no single market secret to discover, no single correct way to trade the markets. Those seeking the one true answer to the markets haven't even gotten as far as asking the right question, let alone getting the right answer.

There are a million ways to make money in the markets. Unfortunately, they are all very difficult to find. But there are many, many ways to succeed. Some traders, such as Rogers, succeed using only fundamental analysis; others, such as Schwartz, succeed using only technical analysis; and still others use a combination of the two. Some traders succeed holding positions for months, or even years, while others succeed on a time scale measured in minutes. Market success is a matter of finding the methodology that is *right for you*—and it will be different for everyone—not a matter of finding the *one true* methodology.

Chapter Three

Trading Your Own Personality

~

In the previous chapter, we established that there is no one path that will lead to success as a trader. This insight points to an essential element of trading success. If you get nothing else out of reading this book than the one following principle, it will still have been a very worthwhile endeavor:

Successful traders find a methodology that fits their personality.

So, while there is no single correct way to trade the markets, in order to be successful, you need to find the one way that is right for you—a methodology that suits your personality. It is the one thing that all the successful traders I have ever interviewed had in common: They all developed a trading style that was consistent with their personality and beliefs. This observation seems very logical to the point of even sounding obvious. You might wonder, "Doesn't everyone trade in line with their personality?"

Well, actually, no, they don't. Schwartz spent nearly a decade trying to adapt fundamental analysis to trading markets, an approach that was very poorly attuned to his personality. It led to tying his ego to his fundamentally derived market opinions. Speaking of this early period, Schwartz said, "Although I steadily earned good salaries, I was still almost broke because I consistently lost money in the market."

It was not until Schwartz immersed himself in technical analysis that he became successful. Technical analysis gave Schwartz a methodology that allowed him to get out of trades quickly when he was wrong. If he got out of a losing trade, there were always lots of other trades in front of him. As Schwartz explained, "By living the philosophy that my winners are always in front of me, it was not so painful to take a loss. If I make a mistake, so what?" He had found a methodology that was a much better personal fit. The point here is not that technical analysis is better than fundamental analysis, but rather that technical analysis was the better methodology for Schwartz. For other traders, such as Jim Rogers, the reverse would be true.

You would be surprised by the number of people who waste time and money trying to fit their personality into a trading method that is not suited for them. There are traders who have innate skills in creating computerized trading systems that do well in the markets, but then feel a compulsion to intervene with discretionary trades—often sabotaging their own systems. There are traders who are naturally attuned to ascertaining long-term market trends, but who get bored staying with a position for a long time and then make short-term trades that lose money. People stray from methodologies that best suit their personality and skills all the time.

Paul Tudor Jones

Let me illustrate what I mean by trading to fit your personality by again contrasting two of the traders I interviewed. The first is Paul Tudor Jones, one of the great futures traders of our time. I interviewed Jones about a half year after the October 1987 stock market crash. In that month, which was catastrophic for many, Jones had an incredible 62 percent return. Moreover, he had just nearly achieved five consecutive years of triple-digit returns. I say "nearly" because in one of those years his fund was up only 99 percent.

When I arranged to interview Jones, he scheduled a time within market hours. I was a bit concerned about this because I knew Jones was a very active trader. Sure enough, when I was ushered into his office, he was shouting an order into one of the speakerphones that directly connected him to the trading floors. This was back in the days before electronic trading, when futures were traded in the pits on the exchange floors.

I waited until he had finished placing his order before speaking. I explained that I didn't want to interrupt his trading and suggested that perhaps we should delay the interview until after all the markets had closed.

"No problem," Jones answered. "Let's go."

As he was responding to my interview questions, Jones kept his eyes on the large quote monitors spread across the room, intermittently shouting orders to the exchange floor in a particularly frenetic style, the trading equivalent of a professional tennis player aggressively returning a volley: "Buy 300 December crude at even! Go, go, go! Are we in? Speak to me!" All during this time, he was also taking phone calls and speaking to staff members popping into his office with market information and questions.

Gil Blake

Keep the image of Paul Tudor Jones trading in his office in mind as we take a look at a very different trader, Gil Blake.

Ironically, Blake became involved in trading in an effort to demonstrate to a colleague that the markets were random and that he was wasting his time if he thought he could gain any advantage through market timing. At the time, Blake was working as the CFO for a company. One day a colleague showed Blake research he had done that suggested he would be better off switching out of a municipal bond fund he held anytime it started to go down and switching back in when it started to go up. He asked Blake for his advice.

Blake was skeptical. "I don't think the markets work that way," he told his friend. "Have you ever read *A Random Walk Down Wall Street*? The problem is that you don't have enough data. Get more data, and I bet you'll find this is not something you could make money on over the long run."

When Blake got the additional data, he discovered his initial skepticism was unwarranted. There clearly was evidence of nonrandom persistence in fund prices. Moreover, the more research he did, the more decisive were the nonrandom patterns in fund prices he discovered. Blake became so convinced that profitable price patterns existed that he quit his job so that he could devote full time to price research. As Blake describes this early period in his trading career, "I practically lived at the local library, extracting years of data on perhaps a hundred mutual funds off the microfilm machine." Blake discovered high-probability patterns that were so enticing that he took out multiple second mortgages on his home to increase his trading stake.

Blake's track record was incredibly consistent. I interviewed him 12 years after he started. He had averaged a 45 percent return per year during that time, with his worst year being a 24 percent gain with all positive months. In fact, he had only five negative months during the entire 12 years. He had one streak of 65 consecutive winning months.

Despite his enormous success, Blake had no desire to create a money management business or grow beyond a one-man operation. He did his trading from the bedroom of his house. He turned down offers to manage money, with the exception of a few friends and family accounts.

Comparing Jones and Blake

Now compare Jones and Blake. Can you imagine Jones spending months in the library going through prices on microfilm and trading once a day from his bedroom? Or could you imagine Blake trading in the chaotic environment in which Jones thrives? There is something jarring about these images. They just don't fit. Jones and Blake have succeeded spectacularly because they have utilized methodologies that suit their personalities. But if they had chosen an approach that was out of sync with their natural character (such as each other's methodology), the results would probably have been very different.

~

If I try to teach you what I do, you will fail because you are not me. If you hang around me, you will observe what I do, and you may pick up some good habits. But there are a lot of things you will want to do differently.

Colm O'Shea

The essential message is that traders must find a methodology that fits their own beliefs and talents. A sound methodology that is very successful for one trader can be a poor fit and a losing strategy for another trader. Colm O'Shea, one of the global macro managers I interviewed, lucidly expressed this concept in answer to the question of whether trading skill could be taught: "If I try to teach you what I do, you will fail because you are not me. If you hang around me, you will observe what I do, and you may pick up some good habits. But there are a lot of things you will want to do differently. A good friend of mine, who sat next to me for several years, is now managing lots of money at another hedge fund and doing very well. But he is not the same as me. What he learned was not to become me. He became something else. He became him."

Personality and Trading Systems

The idea that using a methodology that suits your personality is an essential component of trading success also helps explain why most people lose money using trading systems they bought. Why is that true? Is it because most trading systems don't work on data not used in their development? I am not implying that. Actually, I have no idea what percentage of trading systems sold to the public provide a market edge. But even if I assumed that more than 50 percent of the systems sold would be profitable if applied as instructed, I would still expect over 90 percent of the buyers of those systems to lose money trading them.

Why? Because every trading system, regardless of the strategy employed, is going to hit periods when it does poorly. Now, if you buy a system, by definition, it has nothing to do with your personality or beliefs. In many, if not most, cases, you won't even have any idea what drives the system's signals. Consequently, the first time the system hits a bad period, you are not going to have the confidence to stay with the system, and you will stop trading it. That is why, invariably, most people who buy systems will end up losing: They will stop using the system when it goes through a bad period, and they won't be there when the system recovers.

Chapter Four

The Need for an Edge

Money Management Is Not Enough

There is a Wall Street adage that says, "Even a poor trading system could make money with good money management." Have you heard that saying before? Well, if you have, forget it, because it is really one of the stupidest things that has ever been said about trading. If you believe that good money management can salvage a poor system or methodology, I invite you to go to a casino, walk over to a roulette wheel, use your best money management system to bet, and see how well that works out for you. In fact, if you asked a hundred mathematicians the question, "I have $1,000 that I want to bet in roulette—what is the optimal betting strategy I should use?," all 100 should give you the same answer: Take the entire $1,000 and place it on red or black (or on odd or even) for one spin, and then, win or lose, walk away. That betting strategy will give you the highest probability of being a winner in roulette.[1]

Of course, your odds of winning are still less than 50 percent—47.37 percent, to be exact, for a wheel with a double zero—but your negative edge will be smallest for one spin. The more times you play, the greater the probability that you will lose. And if you play long enough, it is a mathematical certainty you will lose. So the point is that if you don't have an edge (implying you have a negative edge), then the optimal money management strategy is to bet it all at once—the epitome of bad money management. Money management cannot save you if you don't have an edge. It is helpful in mitigating losses and preserving capital only if you do have an edge.

So, it's not enough to have money management; you also need to have an edge. Having an edge means that you have a method.

So, it's not enough to have money management; you also need to have an edge. Having an edge means that you have a method. No trader I ever interviewed for any of the *Market Wizards* books when asked how he did what he did gave a response like, "I look at the screen, and if bonds look good, I'll buy some." None of them approached trading with a cavalier, shoot-from-the-hip attitude. They all had a specific methodology. Some of them could describe their methodology in very specific, almost step-by-step terms. Others described their approach in more general terms. But it was clear they all had a specific methodology.

So what exactly is your methodology? If you can't answer that question, you are not ready to be risking money in the markets. If you can answer that question, the next question is, "Does your trading method provide an edge?" If you are unsure about the answer, again, you are not ready to be risking money in the markets. Successful traders are confident that their methodology provides an edge.

An Edge Is Not Enough

Just as money management is insufficient without an edge, an edge is insufficient without money management. You need both. Monroe Trout, who achieved one of the best long-term return/risk records ever recorded, nicely summarized this concept. When I asked him what trading rules he lived by, he replied, "Make sure you have the edge. Know what your edge is. Have rigid risk control rules. . . . To make money, you need to have an edge and employ good money management. Good money management alone isn't going to increase your edge at all. If your system isn't any good, you're still going to lose money, no matter how effective your money management rules are. But if you have an approach that makes money, then money management can make the difference between success and failure." We explore the money management part of the equation in Chapter 8.

Chapter Five

The Importance of Hard Work

I INTERVIEWED MARTY SCHWARTZ IN the evening after a long trading day. He was in the middle of doing his daily market analysis in preparation for the next day. It was a lengthy interview, and we finished quite late. Schwartz was visibly tired. But he wasn't about to call it a day. He still had to complete his daily market analysis routine. As he explained, "My attitude is that I always want to be better prepared than someone I'm competing against. The way I prepare myself is by doing my work each night."

**My attitude is that I always want
to be better prepared than someone I'm
competing against. The way I prepare myself
is by doing my work each night.**

Marty Schwartz

I was amazed to find that so many of the great traders I interviewed were workaholics. Although I could provide many examples, we will take a look at just two of the traders I interviewed to provide a flavor of the work ethic that typifies highly successful traders.

David Shaw

David Shaw is the founder of D.E. Shaw, one of the most successful quantitative trading firms in the world. Shaw assembled scores of the country's most brilliant mathematicians, physicists, and computer scientists to develop multiple computer models that in combination could extract consistent profits from the markets by exploiting pricing discrepancies among different securities. The entire trading strategy is exceedingly complex, trading thousands of financial instruments, including equities, warrants, options, and convertible bonds on all the major global markets. You would think that heading up this massive trading operation and directing and supervising ongoing research of a large team of brilliant quantitative scientists would be more than enough work for any individual. But, apparently, it was not enough for David Shaw.

Over the years, Shaw's firm has also incubated and spun off a number of other companies, including Juno Online Services (subsequently merged into United Online), a financial technology company sold to Merrill Lynch, an online brokerage firm, and a market-making operation, among others. In addition, Shaw became heavily involved in computational biochemistry, keeping current on the developing research and providing venture capital to several firms in this field. (Shaw eventually turned over the management of D.E. Shaw to a management team so that he could devote full time to research and development in the field of computational biochemistry.) In addition to all these pursuits, Shaw also served on President Bill Clinton's Committee of Advisors on Science and Technology and chaired the Panel on Educational Technology. It is hard to contemplate how one person could do all of this. I asked Shaw if he ever took any vacation time, and he answered, "Not much. When I take a vacation, I find I need a few hours of work each day just to keep myself sane."

John Bender

John Bender was a brilliant options trader who managed money for George Soros's Quantum Fund and who also traded his own fund. When I interviewed him in 1999, his fund had an average annual compounded return of 33 percent with a maximum drawdown of only 6 percent. In the following year (the last year of the fund), his fund registered an astounding 269 percent return, as the option trades Bender had positioned in anticipation of a major top in the stock market proved immensely profitable. He closed the fund in 2000 because he had suffered a brain aneurysm. Bender spent the next decade buying up huge tracts of rainforest acreage and establishing a wildlife preserve in Costa Rica. Sadly, Bender suffered from bipolar disorder and committed suicide in 2010 during one of his depressive states.[1]

While Bender was trading, he was probably most active in the Japanese options market. He would then stay up and trade the European options markets and, typically, extend his day into the U.S. trading session. It would be normal for Bender to spend as much as 20 hours a day trading. I mention this example not as a recommendation on how to live your life, but as an illustration of the types of extremes to which some of the Market Wizards carried hard work.

The Paradox

Now here is the irony. Why are so many people attracted to trading? Because it seems like an easy way to make a lot of money. But the fact is that the people who are really successful in trading are tremendously hard workers. This dichotomy between perception and reality as it pertains to trading success and work leads to the following paradox. You'll grant me that no sane person would think of going into a bookstore (assuming you could still find one these days), walking over to the medical books section, finding a book titled *Techniques of Brain Surgery*, studying it over the weekend, and then Monday morning walking into a hospital operating room believing he was ready to perform brain surgery. The operative word here is *sane*—that is, no sane person would think that way.

Yet how many people do you know who would think there was absolutely nothing unusual about going into a bookstore, walking to the business book section, buying a book called *How I Made $1,000,000 in the Stock Market Last Year*, reading it over the weekend, and then Monday morning believing that they can beat the market professionals at their own game. The line of reasoning in both examples is really quite similar. But, while it is obvious that the thinking in the brain surgery scenario is deranged, many people see nothing odd about the thought process in the second scenario. Why such a dichotomy?

But the fact is: The people who are really successful in trading are tremendously hard workers.

Well, this is one paradox that I believe has a satisfactory explanation. Trading is probably the world's only profession in which a rank amateur, the person who knows absolutely nothing, has a 50–50 chance of being right in the beginning. Why? Because there are only two things you can do in trading: You can buy or you can sell. And, as a matter of probability, some significant percentage of people will be right more than 50 percent of the time—at least in the beginning.

As an analogy, if you have 1,000 people toss 10 coins in the air, on average, nearly 30 percent of them will toss 60 percent or more heads. In the coin toss experiment, the 60 percent-plus heads flippers will realize their results are a matter of luck and not due to any innate skill in tossing heads. But when it comes to trading, the amateur traders who are right more than 50 percent of the time when they are starting out will attribute their success to their superior decision-making skills, rather than simply being a matter of chance. The fact that it is possible to achieve short-term trading success by pure luck beguiles people into thinking that trading is a lot easier than it is. It fools people into believing that they possess trading skill.

The same misperception can't happen in any other profession. If you never trained as a surgeon, the odds of your performing successful brain surgery are zero. If you have never played the violin, the odds of your getting up in front of the New York Philharmonic and playing a successful solo are zero. In any profession you consider, the odds of even short-term success for the untrained beginner are zero. It is just a quirk of trading that you could be successful for the short term without knowing anything, and that possibility fools people.

Chapter Six

Good Trading Should Be Effortless

〜

IN READING THIS CHAPTER'S title you are probably think-ing, "Wait a minute. In the last chapter you told us success-ful trading involves a lot of hard work. Now you are saying good trading is effortless. Make up your mind. Which is it?"

〜

The hard work in trading comes in the preparation. The actual process of trading, however, should be effortless.

There is no contradiction. It is the difference between preparation and process. The hard work in trading comes in the preparation. The actual process of trading, however, should be effortless. I will use a running analogy. Picture someone who is completely out of shape, whose longest pedestrian excursions are from the couch to the refrigerator, trying to run one mile in 10 minutes. Now, picture a world-class runner running a marathon one mile after another, easy as can be, at a sub-5-minute per mile pace. Who is doing more hard work? Who is more successful? Well, clearly the out-of-shape runner is doing more hard work, but the world-class runner is much more successful. The world-class runner, however, didn't get to this level of proficiency by just getting off the couch one day and going for one short run. He has been training hard for many years. So, his hard work came in the preparation. When he is performing successfully, however, the actual process of running should be effortless; he will run his best races when he is running effortlessly. The same concept would apply to many other endeavors. Writers achieve their best work when the writing comes effortlessly; musicians perform best when their playing comes effortlessly.

The same principles apply in trading. If trading is going well, it will seem effortless. If trading is not going well, you can't force it right by working harder. If you are in a particularly bad trading period, when nearly every decision you make seems to be wrong, trying harder won't help. It will probably only make matters worse. You can work harder in doing more research. You can work harder in trying to figure out what's going wrong. But you can't work harder at trading. If you are out of sync with the markets, trying harder is often likely to make matters even worse. So if trying harder is not the solution for handling a losing streak, what is? We will address this question in the next chapter.

Zen and the Art of Trading

There was an interview I did in which the theme of good trading being effortless came up prominently. Unfortunately, it was an interview I could not include in one of my books. Let me explain.

People often wonder how I get the traders in my books to agree to be interviewed. One of the things I do to allay the concerns of potential interview subjects is to assure them that they will have a chance to review the finished chapter before I submit the manuscript to the publisher. I also tell them that I will not use the chapter unless they approve it. I believe these assurances are not only helpful in getting traders to participate, but also aid in their being more open and free in their responses to my questions. I am sure that if the traders I interviewed had no control over the process, they would self-censor every reply before it was immortalized in print. Although my promise not to publish the interview without approval serves some very useful purposes, it can also backfire. I can spend weeks honing 200 pages of raw transcript into a 25-page chapter only to have the interview subject decline to let me use it. Fortunately, this has happened only twice.

On one of these occasions I did a fairly eclectic interview for *The New Market Wizards*. The scope of the interview was quite unusual, including such topics as dreams and trading, precognition and trading, and Zen and trading. I wrote it all up, and I thought the end result was pretty good. As agreed, I sent the completed chapter to the trader for his review and approval. About a week later, he called me.

"I read the interview," he said. "It was quite interesting. . . ." I sensed a "but" coming. "But," he continued, "you can't use it." It turned out that he had decided to go into the business of advising corporations on currency hedging and had hired a business manager to help develop and market the service. The business manager had read the interview and saw all this stuff about dreams and trading, and Zen and trading, and he quickly decided the material was not conducive to projecting the desired corporate image. "No way," said the business manager, and "No way," said the trader.

Trying to salvage something from an impending complete loss, I said, "There is a small section that I think has a very important message, and I would hate to lose it. Just let me use this one section, and I won't identify you by name."

He agreed. As a result, there is a two-page chapter in *The New Market Wizards* called "Zen and the Art of Trading." In it, the trader asks me, "Did you ever read *Zen and the Art of Archery?*"

"No, I have to admit, I missed that one," I replied.

The essence of the idea is that you have to learn to let the arrow shoot itself. . . . In trading, just as in archery, whenever there is effort, force, straining, struggling, or trying, it's wrong. . . . The perfect trade is one that requires no effort.

A trader

He continued earnestly, ignoring my glib response, "The essence of the idea is that you have to learn to let the arrow shoot itself. . . . In trading, just as in archery, whenever there is effort, force, straining, struggling, or trying, it's wrong. . . . The perfect trade is one that requires no effort."

If you are a trader, you will recognize the truth in every one of those words.

Chapter Seven

The Worst of Times, the Best of Times

~

When Everything Is Going Wrong

Okay, good trading should be effortless. But what do you do when you hit prolonged periods when trading is a struggle? How do you handle the periods when almost everything seems to be going wrong and you are in a steadily deepening drawdown? This question came up in multiple interviews. Even great traders can experience demoralizing losing periods. The Market Wizards were quite consistent in the advice they offered about handling difficult losing periods. They had two basic recommendations:

1. **Reduce your trading size**. Paul Tudor Jones said, "When I am trading poorly, I keep reducing my position size. That way, I will be trading my smallest position size when my trading is worst."

   Ed Seykota, a pioneer in systematic futures trading who achieved astounding cumulative returns, offered similar advice when I asked him if he had locked away several million dollars to avoid the Jesse Livermore experience. (Livermore was a famous speculator of the early twentieth century who made and lost several fortunes.) Seykota replied that a better alternative was to "Keep reducing risks during equity drawdowns. That way you will approach your safe money asymptotically and have a gentle financial and emotional touchdown."

   Marty Schwartz will cut his trading size to a fifth or even a tenth of normal if he experiences losses that shake his confidence. "After a devastating loss," Schwartz said, "I always play very small and try to get black ink, black ink. . . . And it works." Schwartz recalls that after he took an unusually large $600,000 hit in his account on November 4, 1982, he responded by drastically reducing his trading size, piecing together many small gains and finishing the month with only a $57,000 loss.

Randy McKay, who parlayed an initial $2,000 trading stake into tens of millions in profit by the time I interviewed him 20 years later, is even more extreme in reducing his position size when he is in a losing streak. "I'll keep on reducing my trading size as long as I'm losing," he says. "I've gone from trading as many as 3,000 contracts per trade to as few as 10 when I was cold, and then back again." He considered this drastic variation in position size as a key element in his trading success.

2. **Stop trading**. Sometimes reducing trading size is simply not enough, and the best remedy to break the downward spiral is to simply stop trading. As Michael Marcus explained, "I think that, in the end, losing begets losing. When you start losing, it touches off negative elements in your psychology; it leads to pessimism. . . . When I have had a bad losing streak, I have been able to say to myself, 'You just can't trade anymore.'"

Richard Dennis, who turned a $400 trading stake into a fortune, estimated by some to be near $200 million at the time of our interview, had a very similar perspective, expressing that losses beyond a certain level will adversely impact the trader's judgment. His straightforward advice: "When you are getting beat to death, get your head out of the mixer."

If you are in a losing streak, the best solution is not trying harder, but rather the exact opposite: Stop trading. Take a break or even a vacation, liquidating all positions or protecting them with stops before you leave. A physical break can serve to interrupt the downward spiral and loss of confidence that can develop during losing periods. Then when you return, ease back into trading, starting small, and gradually increasing if trading has again become effortless.

∾

If you are in a losing streak, the best solution is not trying harder, but rather the exact opposite: Stop trading.

Although traders will know when they are in losing streaks, they may be slow to realize the dimensions of the problem until the loss has far exceeded acceptable levels. They allow losses to mount without changing anything and then suddenly are shocked to realize the magnitude of their drawdown. One way to become cognizant of these persistent losing periods more quickly and in time to take corrective action before excessive damage is done is to plot your equity daily. Marcus offered this advice, noting, "If the trend in your equity is down, that is a sign to cut back and reevaluate."

When Everything Is Great

The flip side of persistent losing periods are times when things are going almost unbelievably well. Oddly enough, these are also times to consider playing smaller. After a particularly strong period of profits, Marty Schwartz will also reduce trading size, just as he does after particularly bad losses, because he notes, "My biggest losses have always followed my largest profits."

I am sure many traders have had a similar experience. The worst drawdowns often follow periods when everything seems to be working perfectly. Why is there a tendency for the worst losses to follow the best performance? One possible explanation is that winning streaks lead to complacency, and complacency leads to sloppy trading. In these strongly winning periods, the trader is least likely to consider what might go wrong, especially worst-case scenarios. An additional explanation is that periods of excellent performance are also likely to be times of particularly high exposure. The moral is: If your portfolio is sailing to new highs almost daily and virtually all your trades are working, watch out! These are the times to guard against complacency and to be extra cautious.

Chapter Eight

Risk Management

~

WHEN I ASKED PAUL TUDOR JONES what was the most important advice he could give to the average trader, he replied,
"Don't focus on making money; focus on protecting what
you have."

Most trading novices believe that trading success is
all about finding a great method for entering trades. The
Market Wizards I interviewed, however, generally agreed
that money management (i.e., risk control) was more important to trading success than the trade selection methodology.
You can do quite well with a mediocre (i.e., slightly better

than random) entry methodology and good money management, but you are likely to eventually go broke with a superior entry methodology and poor money management. The unfortunate reality is that the amount of attention most beginning traders devote to money management is inversely proportional to its importance.

**Don't focus on making money;
focus on protecting what you have.**

Paul Tudor Jones

Uncle Point and Kovner's Dictum

It is instructive to consider how the Market Wizards approach risk control. Marty Schwartz provided perhaps the best succinct description of an effective perspective on risk control. Schwartz's advice is simply, "Know your uncle point." I don't know whether the expression "say uncle" is still used today, but when Schwartz and I were kids, saying "uncle" was the call of surrender to make the pain stop. If two kids were in a fight and one had the other locked in an arm twist, he might demand, "Say 'uncle,'" an understood sign that his opponent was giving up. So what Schwartz is saying is that before you put on a position, you have to know the point at which you will give up to the market because the pain is too great.

Bruce Kovner, the founder of Caxton Associates, was one of the best global macro traders ever. When I interview him, he had been trading for 10 years and had achieved an astounding 87 percent average annualized compounded return during that period. Although this type of return is impossible to maintain, he continued to do very well in the ensuing decades until he retired in 2011. An early trading experience, in which an act of reckless risk caused him to lose half of his accumulated profit in one day, shocked Kovner into a lifelong respect for risk control. (The details of this trade are discussed in Chapter 17.)

One of Kovner's core money management principles was that before he entered any position, he predetermined his exit point based on assessment of where the market should not go if he was right about the trading idea. "That is the only way I can sleep," said Kovner. "I know where I'm getting out before I get in." Why is determining where you will get out before you get in so important? Because before you get into the trade is the last time you have complete objectivity. Once you get into the trade, you lose objectivity, which makes it easier to procrastinate by rationalizing a losing position. By making the loss-limit exit decision before he enters a trade, Kovner ensures a disciplined risk control strategy and removes emotionalism from the money management process.

———————————— ∽ ————————————

I know where I'm getting out before I get in.

Bruce Kovner

———————————————————————————

On a personal note, Kovner's rule about determining where you will get out of a trade before you get in lies at the heart of a trade that I consider my transition point from net losing trader to net winning trader. Ironically, this trade, which I consider one of my best trades ever, was a losing trade. At the time, I had made several prior trading attempts, each time starting with a small stake, wiping out (often because I let the loss on a single trade get out of hand), and then waiting for a while before I made another attempt. The pivotal trade that changed everything involved the deutsche mark, which was the primary European currency prior to the launch of the euro. The deutsche mark had been in a prolonged trading range that formed following an extended decline. Based on my analysis, I believed that the deutsche mark was forming a major price base. I went long within the trading range, anticipating an eventual upside breakout. I simultaneously placed a good-till-canceled sell stop just below the low of the consolidation. I reasoned that if

I was right, the market should not fall to a new low. Several days later, the market started falling, and I was stopped out of my position at a small loss. The great thing was that after I was stopped out, the market decline accelerated sharply. Previously, this type of trade would have wiped out my account; instead I experienced only a minor loss.

If I were asked to provide what I thought was the most important trading advice and restricted to using only 10 words, my reply would be what I would term Kovner's dictum: Know where you will get out before you get in.

How Not to Place Your Stops

Protective stops, or predetermined exit points to limit losses, such as those employed by Schwartz and Kovner, are one of the most effective tools for risk management. However, many traders use such wrongheaded approaches in placing stops that the stop can actually make matters worse. Colm O'Shea, a successful London-based hedge fund manager who managed money for Citigroup, Balyasny Asset Management, and George Soros before starting his own fund, COMAC Capital LLP, recalled how a flawed stop-placement process sabotaged his very first trade.

As a newly hired trader at Citigroup, O'Shea did a fundamental analysis of the UK economy and decided that the rate hikes the forward interest rate market was pricing in were not going to happen. His forecast proved precisely correct. Three months later, there had still not been any rate increase, and short-term interest rate futures had risen 100 points. Although O'Shea had been exactly right, he actually lost money. How did O'Shea manage to lose money despite being right? O'Shea's problem was that he had a longer-term idea about interest rates, but he traded the market with short-term risk constraints. He was continually being stopped out of his position by insignificant adverse price moves because he was too afraid of losing money.

That first trade taught O'Shea that you have to be willing to allow enough risk for the trade to work. O'Shea described how stops should be set and then contrasted that recommended approach to what many traders actually do. "First," said O'Shea, "you need to decide where you are wrong. That determines where the stop level should be. Then you work out how much you are willing to lose on the idea. Last, you divide the amount you're willing to lose by the per-contract loss to the stop point, and that determines your position size. The most common error I see is that people do it backwards. They start with position size. Then they know their pain threshold, and that determines where they place their stop."

Placing a stop too close is also likely to lead to multiple losses. As O'Shea explained, commenting on such traders, "They will get out because their stop is hit, and they are disciplined. But very soon afterwards, they will want to get back in because they don't think they were wrong. That's how day traders in NASDAQ in 2000 and 2001 lost a ton of money. They were disciplined, so they would close out their positions by the end of the day. But they kept repeating the same trading mistake."

Essentially, O'Shea is saying that you should place a stop at a level that disproves your trade premise, as opposed to placing a stop based on your pain level. The market doesn't care about your pain threshold.

An Option to Stops[1]

Although stops can be an invaluable risk management tool, one disadvantage of stops is that the original position can reverse after the stop has been triggered, leaving a trader with a loss on a position that would otherwise have been a gain. Options can be used as an alternative risk management tool that avoids this frustrating scenario at a predetermined fixed cost.

As an example, consider a trader who wants to buy stock XYZ, which is trading at $24, and is willing to risk a maximum loss of $2. The straightforward approach would be to buy the stock and then place a protective stop at $22. (Of course, the loss could still exceed $2 if the stop order is filled below $22.) If the stock declined to $21.80 and then rebounded to $30, the trader would still be left with an approximate $2 per share loss, despite being right in the directional expectation for the stock.

As an alternative to using a stop, the trader could, for example, buy a one-year $22 call on XYZ. In this illustration, we assume the option premium is $3 (or $1 more than the in-the-money amount of the option). If the stock falls below $22 and is still below $22 when the option expires, the trader's loss would be limited to the $3 premium paid for the option, regardless how low the price of the stock falls. If, however, the stock falls below $22 and then rebounds to $30 at the time of the option expiration, the trade would earn a profit of $5 per share (the difference between the $30 expiration price and the $22 strike price, less the $3 premium paid for the option). Whereas, in this scenario, the trader with the stop lost $2 per share, the trader who bought the option had a $5 per share profit ($1 less than the net increase in the share price). Of course, if the stop is not hit, the trader with the stop would be $1 per share better off (the amount by which the premium paid exceeded the in-the-money amount of the option). In-the-money options have the additional advantage of requiring a much lower cash outlay than outright long positions.

So is it better to control position risk with stops or in-the-money options? The answer depends on the preferences of the individual, the liquidity of the options, and the relative expensiveness of options at the time of the trade. The intention here is merely to point out that, in some circumstances, and for some traders, in-the-money options may provide a more attractive risk management tool than stops and therefore should be considered as a possible alternative to stop-protected outright positions.

Risk Management at the Portfolio Level

BlueCrest's flagship fund, a multimanager fund run by Michael Platt, which is designed to keep losses very constrained, has achieved annual returns in excess of 12 percent[2] (after deducting all fees) over a 13-year period, while keeping the peak-to-valley equity drawdown under 5 percent for the entire period. How could BlueCrest deliver double-digit returns over an extended period while keeping the maximum drawdown so low? The answer lies primarily in the portfolio risk management strategy, which tightly limits the amount each manager can lose before capital is withdrawn. Each calendar year starts with a clean slate. Each manager is allowed to lose only up to 3 percent before his allocation is cut by 50 percent. If the manager then loses another 3 percent on the remaining assets, the entire allocation is withdrawn for the year. These rigid risk control rules are designed to keep each manager's maximum loss for the year under 5 percent. (The combination of two successive 3 percent losses is less than a 5 percent loss because the second 3 percent loss is incurred on only 50 percent of the assets.)

You might think that maintaining such tight reins on the maximum allowed loss would also keep returns very subdued. How then has the fund managed to attain annual returns that have averaged two-and-a-half times the size of the single largest equity drawdown for the entire period? The key is that the 3 percent/3 percent risk rule applies only to a manager's starting stake for the year. So while the risk control rules encourage the fund's managers to be very cautious at the outset, managers can take increasingly greater risk as they build a profit cushion. Effectively, a manager can risk the original 3 percent plus any accrued profits for the year before an allocation reduction would be triggered. This structure assures capital preservation while, at the same time, keeping upside potential open-ended by allowing greater risk taking with profits.

Some traders may find that the BlueCrest risk management approach can serve as a model for constraining yearly losses to some preset maximum, while still allowing for greater upside potential. Traders can choose their own appropriate loss levels as thresholds for reducing exposure as well as trading cessation.

Quick Exits When Wrong

The Market Wizards have the ability to get out quickly when they are wrong. When I interviewed Steve Cohen, the founder of SAC Capital and one of the world's most successful traders,[3] he told about a trade in which he was dead wrong. "I went short the stock at $169. The earnings came out and they were just phenomenal—a complete blowout! I got out sharply higher in after-the-close trading, buying back my position at $187. The trade just didn't work. The next day the stock opened at $197. So thank God I covered that night in after-hours trading."

I asked Cohen if he always had the ability to turn on a dime when he was wrong. Cohen answered, "You better be able to do that. This is not a perfect game. I compile statistics on my traders. My best trader makes money only 63 percent of the time. Most [SAC] traders make money only in the 50 to 55 percent range. That means you're going to be wrong a lot. If that's the case, you better make sure your losses are as small as they can be, and that your winners are bigger."

The Trader's Dilemma

Here is a common dilemma, which most traders have faced at one time or another: You have a position that is going against you, but you still believe in the trade. On the one hand, you don't want the loss on the position to get any worse, but, on the other hand, you are concerned that as soon as you get out, the market will turn around in favor of the liquidated trade. This conflict can cause traders to freeze and do nothing as their losses mount. Steve Cohen also had some useful advice about how to handle this type of situation. "If the market is moving against you, and you don't know why, take in half. You can always put in on again. If you do that twice, you've taken in three-quarters of your position. Then what's left is no longer a big deal."

Taking a partial loss is much easier than liquidating the entire position and provides a way to act rather than procrastinate. Yet, most traders will resist the idea of partial liquidation. Why? Because partial liquidation absolutely guarantees that you will be wrong. If the market reverses, then you shouldn't have liquidated anything, and if continues to move further against you, then you should have just liquidated the entire position. No matter what happens, you will be partially wrong. The need to be 100 percent right prevents many traders from considering partial liquidation. Unfortunately, by trying to be 100 percent right, many traders end up being 100 percent wrong. The next time you are undecided between liquidating a losing position and gritting your teeth and riding it out, remember that there is a third possible choice: partial liquidation—an alternative that, as Cohen points out, can be used multiple times on the same position.

When in doubt, get out and get a good night's sleep. I've done that lots of times and the next day everything was clear. . . . While you are in [the position], you can't think. When you get out, then you can think clearly again.

Michael Marcus

Michael Marcus makes the point that when you are confused about what to do with a position, getting out is the best way to gain clarity. "When in doubt," he says, "get out and get a good night's sleep. I've done that lots of times and the next day everything was clear. . . . While you are in [the position], you can't think. When you get out, then you can think clearly again." Marcus's observation that clarity is best obtained when not in the position echoes the reasoning behind Bruce Kovner's advice to decide on an exit before entering a trade.

Underappreciated Reason for Avoiding Large Losses

The direct adverse consequence of letting a loss grow unnecessarily large is quite obvious. However, there is another far less obvious consequence of large losses that can have a major negative impact on equity. Large losses will mentally impede the trader and result in missed winning opportunities. This observation was colorfully expressed by Michael Platt, talking about the aftermath of taking a large loss: "You feel like an idiot, and you're not in the mood to put on anything else. Then the elephant walks past you while your gun's not loaded. It's amazing how annoyingly often that happens. In this game, you want to be there when the great trade comes along. It's the 80/20 rule of life. In trading, 80 percent of your profits come from 20 percent of your ideas."

It's Not Rocket Science

Money management doesn't have to be complex. Although there are entire books devoted just to the subject of money management, I believe a rule so simple that it can be described in a single sentence can get you 90 percent of the way there.

Larry Hite, the cofounder of Mint Investment, one of the largest and most successful commodity trading advisors (CTAs) of the 1980s, was very clear about what he felt was the most important component of the firm's strategy: "The very first rule we live by at Mint is: Never risk more than 1 percent of total equity on any trade." There you have it: effective money management in just one sentence. As Hite elaborated, "By only risking 1 percent, I am indifferent to any individual trade." This type of simple rule works because it prevents any single bad trade from doing much damage. You may still lose money trading, but you won't be knocked out of the game because of one or a few bad trades that are allowed to accumulate losses without limit—a painful outcome experienced by many traders, even those with effective trade entry methodologies.

There is nothing magical about the 1 percent limit; you could use 0.5 percent, or 2 percent, or whatever number is most appropriate for your strategy. The key point is that there is a strict loss limit on every trade. Effective money management is not a matter of complexity, but rather a matter of discipline. Even simple risk control rules will probably work fine, as long as you have the discipline to follow them.

Chapter Nine

Discipline

WHEN I ASKED THE Market Wizards what differentiated them from the majority of traders, the most common reply I got was "discipline." Now, the need for discipline is one of those items of trading advice that you have probably heard so often before that if I just mention it here again, you'll ignore it. Rules are boring and are quickly forgotten, while stories have the potential to capture interest and be remembered. So instead of just repeating the rule about the need for discipline in trading, let me instead tell you a story about discipline, which I hope you will remember the next time you are at the brink of letting your discipline in the markets lapse. My favorite story about discipline in the interviews I've conducted concerns Randy McKay, a very successful discretionary trader who began his trading career with the birth of currency futures trading.

McKay's Lapse of Discipline

McKay's career path got off to a very inauspicious start. He flunked out of college in 1968—six Fs due to lack of attendance did the trick. The year 1968 was near the height of the Vietnam War, and soon after losing his college deferment, McKay was drafted by the Marines. (Although the Marines don't normally draft recruits, there were two months in 1968 when they were allotted a small portion of draftees.) When McKay returned from Vietnam in 1970, his brother, who was a broker on the Chicago Mercantile Exchange (CME), got him a job as a runner on the floor. The job allowed McKay to work in the morning and attend college classes in the late afternoon and evening.

McKay had no intention of becoming a trader. But just as he was finishing college in 1972, the CME launched a subdivision, the International Monetary Market (IMM), to trade currencies. In an effort to try to generate trading activity in the new currency futures contracts, the CME gave away free IMM seats to all existing members. McKay's brother had no need for the seat at the time, and he asked Randy if he would like to use it in the interim. In that initial year of currency futures trading, these markets were so inactive that floor traders in the currency pit spent more time playing chess or checkers or reading the newspaper than trading. McKay found that he had a knack for trading. He was successful in his first year and then made more money in each successive year.

In order to provide context, it is important to make clear that McKay was a very disciplined trader. Perhaps the best illustration of this point was his experience in the aftermath of the November 1978 Carter dollar rescue plan. The dollar had been sliding steadily against all the major currencies all year long. Then on a weekend in November, with major currencies near highs against the dollar, the Carter administration announced a plan to support the dollar. This announcement caught the market by surprise and triggered a huge downside gap in foreign currencies.

At the time, McKay was positioned heavily long in the British pound. Monday morning, British pound futures opened locked limit down.[1] Although futures were locked limit down (a 600-point decline) on the Monday opening, it was possible to trade currencies on the interbank market, which instantly moved to an equilibrium price and traded freely. McKay liquidated his long pound position Monday morning on the interbank market, which was trading 1,800 points lower, equivalent to about three consecutive limit-down price moves in futures.

I asked McKay, "In catastrophic situations, when a surprise news event causes futures to lock at the daily limit and the cash market to immediately move the equivalent of several limit days in futures, do you find that you're generally better off getting out right away, as opposed to taking your chances by waiting until the futures market trades freely?"

When I get hurt in the market, I get the hell out. It doesn't matter at all where the market is trading. I just get out, because I believe that once you are hurt in the markets, your decisions are going to be far less objective than they are when you're doing well.

Randy McKay

McKay's reply to this question left little doubt about where he stood on the question of discipline. "There's a principle I follow that never allows me to even make that decision," McKay said. "When I get hurt in the market, I get the hell out. It doesn't matter at all where the market is trading. I just get out, because I believe that once you are hurt in the markets, your decisions are going to be far less objective than they are when you're doing well. And if the market had rallied 1,800 points that day to close higher, I couldn't have cared less. If you stick around when the market is severely against you, sooner or later they're going to carry you out."

This trade was by far McKay's largest loss up to that point, costing him $1.5 million. I asked what emotions he felt at the time. McKay had no regrets. "As long as you're in the position," he said, "there's tremendous anxiety. Once you get out, you begin to forget about it. If you can't put it out of your mind, you can't trade."

So clearly, McKay was a disciplined trader. Now let's fast-forward 10 years to McKay's "next-to-last trade." In his last trade, McKay was going to reach his goal of making $50 million in the markets. This next-to-last trade was supposed to get McKay close enough to his target so that one more strong trade would achieve his goal. That is not quite how things worked out, however. The trade involved a huge long position in the Canadian dollar. The currency had broken through the psychologically critical 80-cent barrier, and McKay was convinced the market was going much higher. As the market moved in his favor, McKay added to his longs, ultimately amassing a 2,000-contract long position.

At the time, McKay was having a house built in Jamaica and would travel there every few weeks to supervise the construction. One Sunday evening, before he rushed off to the airport to catch his connecting flight to Miami, McKay stopped to check the quote screen. He cared about only one position: the Canadian dollar. He looked at the screen and was momentarily shocked. The Canadian dollar was down exactly 100 points! He was late for his flight, and the limo was waiting. *The Canadian dollar rarely moves 20 points in the overnight session, let alone 100 points; it must be a bad quote,* thought McKay. He decided that the market was really unchanged and that the hundreds digit in the quote was off by one. With that rationalization in mind, McKay rushed off for the airport.

It turned out that the quote that evening had not been an error. The market was down 100 points at the time, and by the next morning, it was down 150 points from the IMM Friday close. What had happened was that, with the Canadian election a month away, a poll had come out showing that the liberal candidate—who held some extreme views, including support for an independent Québec, and who had been thought to have no chance of winning—had closed most of the gap versus his opponent. Overnight, the impending election had gone from a foregone conclusion to a toss-up.

To make matters worse, although construction was sufficiently complete for McKay to stay at his new house, phones had not yet been installed. We are talking pre–mobile phone days here. So McKay had to drive to the nearest hotel and stand in line to use the pay phone. By the time he got through to his floor clerk, his Canadian dollar position was down $3 million. Since by that time the market was down so much, McKay got out of only about 20 percent of his position. The Canadian dollar, however, continued its plunge. A few days later, McKay was down $7 million. Once he realized the extent of his loss, he exclaimed to his clerk, "Get me out of everything!"

So here was an experienced trader who committed a momentary lapse of discipline by assuming that an unexpected price decline was due to a bad quote rather than being real—an expediency fostered by concern over being late for his flight—and it cost him $7 million. It is truly amazing how the market will not let traders get away with even a momentary lapse of discipline. The next time you find yourself tempted to ease up on discipline and violate one of your own trading or risk control rules, think of McKay.

Chapter Ten

Independence

~

I<small>T SHOULD COME AS</small> no surprise that highly successful traders are independent. Michael Marcus commented on the need for independence. "You have to follow your own light," he said. ". . . As long as you stick to your own style, you get the good and bad in your own approach. When you try to incorporate someone else's style, you often end up with the worst of both styles."

A Personal Story

I have often found that listening to other people's advice and opinions can be detrimental to one's trading health.

One experience stands out as a perfect illustration. As I go through this story, you may think I may be tweaking it a little bit to make it fit, because the events seem to line up so perfectly, but I can assure you that all the events are described exactly as they occurred.

After I had written *Market Wizards,* one of the traders I interviewed for that book—I won't mention his name here—would call me periodically to discuss the markets. At the time, in addition to being a director of futures research, I was also the firm's technical analyst for the futures markets. This trader was interested in my technical reading of the various futures markets. I was baffled why he would want my opinion when he was a much better trader than I was. For all I knew, maybe he called so that he could fade my opinions on the markets. That made as much sense as anything else.

One morning, this trader called and started going through the markets, asking my opinion. He got to the Japanese yen. At the time, I had been in a poor trading streak and had greatly pared down the positions in my account. The only market I had a strong opinion about was the Japanese yen. "I think the yen is going lower," I said. "The market has had a sharp downswing followed by a very tight consolidation. In my experience, when you have that combined pattern, the market usually goes down again."

The trader then went on to give me 58 reasons why I was wrong. This oscillator was oversold and that oscillator was oversold, and so on. "You're probably right," I said. "It's just an opinion."

Even back then, which was over 20 years ago, I knew enough not to listen to anybody's opinion. But here's the thing: I had to travel to Washington, D.C., that afternoon, and I was going to be gone for a couple of days. I had a very busy schedule and knew that I wouldn't have time to watch the markets. I thought, *I haven't been doing so great lately. I have one significant position left. Do I really want to fade one of the best traders I know*—and here is where the rationalization comes in; wait for it—*when I won't even be able to watch the market?* So against my better judgment, I walked over to the after-hours trading desk and put in an order to liquidate my position. It was a rationalization because I could have just put in a protective stop order. I didn't need to be able to watch the market to prudently keep the position.

I am sure you will not be surprised to learn that when I returned from my trip several days later, the yen was down several hundred points. But here is where you have to believe me. On that same day, the trader called me. Although I was quite curious about his opinion on the yen now that it had fallen sharply in exact contradiction to his opinion in our last conversation, I wasn't going to be so gauche as to raise the subject. But then he said, "What do you think of the yen?"

Playing dumb as if just reminded about our last conversation on this market, I said, "Ah yes, the yen. Are you still long?"

He exclaimed over the phone, "Long? I am short!"

The point is that if you listen to anyone else's opinion, no matter how skillful or smart the trader might be, I guarantee it is going to end badly.

What I didn't mention was that he is a very short-term trader. For him, a long-term trade might be a day, while for me a short-term trade might be two weeks. So, when he talked to me, he was indeed bullish. He was looking for a short-term (read: intraday) bounce. But when the market didn't behave as he expected, he decided he was on the wrong side, liquidated his long, went short, and made 200 points—whereas I, who was right all along, made nothing. The point is that if you listen to anyone else's opinion, no matter how skillful or smart the trader might be, I guarantee it is going to end badly. You just cannot get ahead by listening to other people's opinions. As Michael Marcus says, "You have to follow your own light."

Chapter Eleven

Confidence

W HEN I ASKED PAUL TUDOR JONES whether he kept his own money in his own funds, he answered, "Eighty-five percent of my net worth is invested in my own funds." Why such a large portion? Because in his own words, "I believe that is the safest place in the world for it." This comment was made by a futures trader. In Jones's view, keeping almost all his net worth in his own futures trading fund was the safest investment he could make. What does that tell you? It tells you that he has a tremendous amount of confidence in his ability to manage money.

Monroe Trout, another futures trader, did Paul Tudor Jones one better. He told me he kept 95 percent of his money in his own funds. Some traders were so confident in their approach that they exceeded 100 percent of their net worth invested in their own strategy. In his early years of trading, Gil Blake took out four successive second mortgages over a three-year period (which he was able to do because housing prices were rising quickly) so that he could increase his trading stake. When I asked Blake if he had any reticence about borrowing money to trade, he answered, "No, because the odds were so favorable. Of course, I had to overcome the conventional wisdom. If you tell someone that you are taking out a second mortgage to trade, the responses are hardly supportive. After a while, I just stopped mentioning this detail to others."

Most people would view the large percentage of their net worth that these traders placed in their own funds or trading accounts as high-risk behavior. But that is definitely not how these traders viewed it. On the contrary, as their comments reflect, they placed such a large percentage of their assets in their own trading strategy because they considered it to be a safe investment—a perspective that reflects the high level of confidence they had in their own approach and their ability to manage money.

Indeed, I have found that confidence is one of the most consistent traits exhibited by the successful traders I have interviewed.

This observation leads to a critical question: Are these traders successful because they are confident or are they confident because they are successful? Although it is impossible to definitively answer these two-way cause-and-effect questions, I believe both cause-and-effect directions are true. Certainly, their success in trading led to confidence, but I also believe that their confidence led to trading success. Indeed, I have found that confidence is one of the most consistent traits exhibited by the successful traders I have interviewed.

One way to gauge whether you will be successful as a trader is whether you are confident that you will succeed. Only you can decide on your level of confidence. How will you know when you are confident enough to succeed as a trader? Based on the interviews I have done, all I can say is that you will know when you are there. If you are unsure, you are not there yet, and you need to be aware of that lack of absolute confidence and move more cautiously in committing risk capital. One sure sign that you lack confidence is seeking the advice of others.

Chapter Twelve

Losing Is Part
of the Game

―~―

The Link between Confidence and
Taking Losses

Closely related to confidence is the idea that losing is part
of the game. Linda Raschke exemplifies the mind-set associ-
ated with this perspective. Raschke initially enjoyed a successful career as a floor trader before injuries sustained in a
horse-riding accident forced her to abandon floor trading
and trade from an office instead. Raschke then continued to

be a consistently profitable trader in her ensuing years as an off-the-floor trader.

At one point in our interview, Raschke said, "It never bothered me to lose, because I always knew that I would make it right back." Superficially, that might sound like an arrogant, egotistical comment. But that is not at all in keeping with Raschke's personality. She is not bragging about her trading. Effectively, what Raschke is really saying is: "I have a methodology that I know is going to win in the long run. Along the way there are going to be some losses. If I lose now, I will win subsequently. As long as I stick with my methodology and keep doing what I am doing, I am going to come out ahead." She is saying that losing is part of the process and that a trader needs to understand that to be successful.

Now, if you know you have won the game of trading before you start, then there is no problem taking a loss, because you understand that is just part of the way of getting to the ultimate gain.

Dr. Van Tharp, a research psychologist I interviewed for *Market Wizards*, had done his own analysis of the difference between winning and losing traders. Dr. Tharp listed a number of critical beliefs he found that top traders shared. Two of these beliefs directly related to the theme of this chapter. First, top traders believed it was okay to lose money in the market. Second, they knew they had won the game before they started. Now, if you know you have won the game of trading before you start, then there is no problem taking a loss, because you understand that is just part of the way of getting to the ultimate gain.

The Rationalization of a Losing Trader

Marty Schwartz described how his transition from a losing trader to a winning trader required accepting that losing was part of the game. He said, "What is the ultimate rationalization of a trader in a losing position? 'I'll get out when I am even.' Why is getting out even so important? Because it protects the ego. I was able to become a winning trader when I was able to say, 'To hell with my ego—making money is more important.'"

If you get out even, you can say, "I wasn't wrong. I didn't make a mistake." That need not to be wrong is exactly why people lose. So, the irony is that amateur traders lose money because they try to avoid losing. Professional traders, however, understand that they need to take losses in order to win. They understand that taking losses is an integral part of the trading process. To win at trading, you need to understand that losing is part of the game.

The Four Types of Trades[1]

Most traders think there are two types of trades: winning trades and losing trades. Actually, there are four types of trades: winning trades and losing trades plus good trades and bad trades. Don't confuse the concepts of winning and losing trades with good and bad trades. A good trade can lose money, and a bad trade can make money. A good trade follows a process that will be profitable (at an acceptable risk) if repeated multiple times, although it can lose money on any individual trade.

Suppose I offer to bet you on coin tosses with a coin you know is fair (your coin and your toss): heads, you pay me $100; tails, I pay you $200. You accept the bet, toss the coin, and it lands on heads. Was that a bad bet? Of course not. It was a good bet that was also a losing bet. But if we repeated that bet numerous times, you would fare very well, and taking the first bet was a correct decision, even though you lost money. Similarly, a losing trade that adheres to a profitable strategy is still a good trade because if similar trades are repeated numerous times, the process will win on balance.

Trading is a matter of probabilities. Even the best trading processes will lose a significant percentage of the time. There is no way of knowing a priori which individual trade will make money. As long as a trade adheres to a process with a positive edge, it is a good trade, regardless of whether it wins or loses, because if similar trades are repeated multiple times, they will come out ahead on average. Conversely, a trade that is taken as a gamble is a bad trade, regardless of whether it wins or loses, because, over time, such trades will lose money. As a betting analogy, a winning slot machine wager is still a bad bet (i.e., trade) because if repeated multiple times, it has a high probability of losing money.

Willing to Lose

You can't win if you are not willing to lose. Bruce Kovner says that one of the most important things Michael Marcus taught him was that "you have to be willing to make mistakes regularly; there is nothing wrong with it. Michael taught me about making your best judgment, being wrong, making your next best judgment, being wrong, making your third best judgment, and then doubling your money."

Chapter Thirteen

Patience

W‌HEN ASKED WHAT HE thought the average trader did wrong, Tom Baldwin, who in the days before electronic trading was the largest individual trader in the Treasury bond pit, replied, "They trade too much. They don't pick their spots selectively enough. When they see the market moving, they want to be in on the action. So, they end up forcing the trade rather than waiting patiently. Patience is an important trait many people don't have."

Century-Old Wisdom

Perhaps the most famous book about trading ever written was *Reminiscences of a Stock Operator* by Edwin Lefèvre, which was published in 1923 and still remains remarkably pertinent now 90 years later. The book is a fictionalized autobiographical account of the trading experiences of a protagonist widely assumed to be Jesse Livermore. The book so accurately captures the mind-set of a trader that I recall when I first read it 35 years ago many people mistakenly assumed Edwin Lefèvre was a pseudonym for Jesse Livermore.

~

There is the plain fool, who does the wrong thing at all times everywhere, but there is the Wall Street fool, who thinks he must trade all the time.

From Reminiscences of a Stock Operator
by Edwin Lefèvre

In *Reminiscences* the narrator states, "There is the plain fool, who does the wrong thing at all times everywhere, but there is the Wall Street fool, who thinks he must trade all the time." Elsewhere, he explains the reasons for the compulsion of traders to trade every day and the consequences of this mind-set: "The desire for constant action irrespective of underlying conditions is responsible for many losses on Wall Street even among the professionals, who feel that they must take home some money every day, as though they were working for regular wages." The message is clear: You need to have the patience to wait for real opportunities and resist the temptation to trade all the time.

A Master of Patience

When I interviewed Michael Marcus, he identified Ed Seykota as the most influential person in transforming him into a successful trader. Seykota was one of the pioneers in the systematic trading of futures and achieved remarkable compounded returns. One of his accounts, which started in 1972 with $5,000, had increased by 250,000 percent by the time I interviewed Seykota in 1988.

One of the most important lessons Marcus learned from Seykota was patience. As Marcus recalls, "One time, he was short silver, and the market kept edging down, a half penny a day, a penny a day. Everyone else seemed bullish, talking about why silver had to go up because it was so cheap, but Ed stayed short. Ed said, 'The trend is down, and I'm going to stay short until the trend changes.' I learned patience from him in the way he followed the trend."

When I interviewed Seykota, I was surprised that he did not have a quote machine on his desk and asked him about it. Seykota wryly replied, "Having a quote machine is like having a slot machine on your desk—you end up feeding it all day long. I get my price data after the close each day." Seykota's systems would give him trade signals when the conditions for a trade were met based on daily price data. Seykota did not even want to know about intraday market gyrations, as they could only provide a temptation to trade more frequently than dictated by his methodology. The dangers of watching every tick are twofold: It can lead to overtrading, and it is likely to increase the chances of prematurely liquidating good positions on insignificant adverse market moves.

The Power of Doing Nothing

The basic idea is that you have to wait for the trading opportunities and resist the natural urge to trade more frequently. Jim Rogers stressed the importance of trading only when you have very strong convictions. "One of the best rules anybody can learn about investing," he said, "is to do nothing, absolutely nothing, unless there is something to do."

When I then asked Rogers whether he always had to have everything line up before taking a position, or whether he might occasionally put on a trade based on his hunch of an impending price move, he answered, "What you just described is a very fast way to the poorhouse. I just wait until there is money lying in the corner, and all I have to do is go over there and pick it up." In other words, until the trade is so obvious that it's like picking money up off the floor, he does nothing. Waiting for such ideal opportunities requires the patience to allow a lot of nonoptimal trades to pass by without participating.

The idea that you don't have to trade was also brought up by Joel Greenblatt, the manager of Gotham Capital, an event-driven hedge fund. During the 10 years of its operation (1985–1994), Gotham realized an average annual compounded return of 50 percent (before incentive fees) with a worst single year of positive 28.5 percent. Greenblatt closed Gotham Capital because assets had grown to the point where they were impeding returns. After an interim of trading only proprietary capital, Greenblatt returned to money management using value-based strategies that could accommodate more capital.

There are no called strikes on Wall Street.

Warren Buffett

As a hobby, Greenblatt has taught a course in the Columbia Business School for many years. In our interview, Greenblatt related the advice he gave students when they asked him what to do with companies whose future earnings were very difficult to predict because of rapid technological changes, new products, or other factors. Greenblatt is a big fan of Warren Buffett and invoked a Buffett aphorism in advising his students how to handle such ambiguous investment situations. "I tell them to skip that company and find a company that they can analyze. It is very important to know what you don't know. As Warren Buffett says, 'There are no called strikes on Wall Street.' You can watch as many pitches as you want and only swing when everything sets up your way."

Claude Debussy said, "Music is the space between the notes." One could also say that successful trading is the space between the trades. Just as the notes not played are important to music, the trades not taken are important to trading success. Kevin Daly, an equity trader I interviewed in *Hedge Fund Market Wizards*, provides a perfect example of this principle. Although, technically speaking, Daly is a long/short equity manager, his total short position is invariably very small—almost always measured in single-digit percentages of assets under management. So, in this sense, Daly is much closer to a long-only equity manager than to a long/short manager. Daly launched his fund in late 1999, only about a half-year before the major stock market top in early 2000. Clearly, this was an unpropitious staring point for a manager whose portfolio primarily consists of long equities. Yet, despite this unfavorable timing, at the time I interviewed Daly, he had managed to achieve a cumulative gross return of 872 percent during an 11-year period in which the Russell 2000 was up only 68 percent and the S&P 500 was actually down 9 percent.

How did Daly achieve such strong returns during a period of near flat stock prices, despite running a portfolio that was predominantly long? Part of the answer is that he was very good at picking stocks that outperformed the indexes. But perhaps the most important factor in explaining Daly's outperformance is that he had the discipline to remain largely in cash during negative market environments, which allowed him to sidestep large drawdowns during two major bear markets. During a time span in which the S&P 500 witnessed two separate occasions where it lost nearly half its value, Daly's largest peak-to-valley drawdown was only 10 percent. The key is that by avoiding large losses by not trading, Daly was able to increase his cumulative return tremendously. Achieving this result necessitated maintaining a very low exposure for much of the extended 2000–2002 bear market. Think of the patience that required. Daly's patience and the trades that he did not take made all the difference.

Mark Weinstein, a trader I interviewed in *Market Wizards*, used an animal kingdom analogy to illustrate the link between patience and good trading: "I also don't lose much on my trades because I wait for the exact right moment. . . . Although the cheetah is the fastest animal in the world and can catch any animal on the plains, it will wait until it is absolutely sure it can catch its prey. It may hide in the bush for a week, waiting for just the right moment. It will wait for a baby antelope, and not just any baby antelope, but preferably one that is sick and lame. Only then, when there is no chance it can lose its prey, does it attack. That, to me, is the epitome of professional trading."

As the foregoing illustrations demonstrate, the Market Wizards wait patiently, doing nothing until there is a sufficiently compelling trade opportunity. The lesson is that if conditions are not right, or the return/risk trade-off is not sufficiently favorable, don't do anything. Beware of taking dubious trades born out of impatience.

Doing nothing is harder than it sounds because it requires resisting the natural human tendency to trade more frequently—a consequence of the addictive nature of trading. William Eckhardt, a long-term successful trader and CTA and former partner of Richard Dennis, who along with Dennis trained the group of CTAs known as the Turtles, explained why trading is addictive. "When behavioral psychologists have compared the relative addictiveness of various reinforcement schedules, they found that intermittent reinforcement—positive and negative dispensed randomly (for example, the rat doesn't know whether it will get pleasure or pain when it hits the bar)—is the most addictive alternative of all, more addictive than positive reinforcement only."

The Wisdom of Sitting

Patience is not only essential in getting into a trade, but also critical in getting out of a trade. Once again quoting from *Reminiscences of a Stock Operator*, "It never was my thinking that made the big money for me. It always was my sitting. Got that? My sitting tight! It is no trick at all to be right on the market. You always find lots of early bulls in bull markets and early bears in bear markets. I've known many men who were right at exactly the right time, and . . . they made no real money out of it. Men who can both be right and sit tight are uncommon."

The theme of what I would call "the importance of sitting" also came up in some of my interviews. One particular proponent of this concept was William Eckhardt, who cited "You can't go broke taking a profit" as one of the most wrongheaded adages about trading. "That's precisely how many traders *do* go broke," said Eckhardt. "While amateurs go broke by taking large losses, professionals go broke by taking small profits." The problem, Eckhardt explains, is that human nature seeks to maximize the *chance* of gain rather than the gain itself. Eckhardt believes that the desire to maximize the number of winning trades works against the trader by encouraging the premature liquidation of good trades. In effect, the need to ensure that a trade will end up in the winning column leads traders to leave a lot of money on the table, thereby severely reducing their total gain in order to increase their winning percentage—a misguided and detrimental goal. As Eckhardt says, "The success rate of trades is the least important performance statistic and may even be inversely related to performance." The message is that regardless of your methodology or the time frame of your trades, you have to allow the good trades to work to their reasonable fruition if you want to pay for the losing trades and still leave a good margin of profit. As Marcus succinctly phrased it, "If you don't stay with your winners, you are not going to be able to pay for the losers."

In summary, patience is a critical quality for a trader—both in getting into and in getting out of trades.

Chapter Fourteen

No Loyalty

LOYALTY IS A GOOD trait—in family, friends, and pets, but not in a trader. For a trader, loyalty is a terrible trait. As a trader, loyalty to an opinion or position can be disastrous. The absence of loyalty is flexibility—the ability to completely change your opinion when warranted. It is the trait Michael Marcus points to when asked what makes him different from most traders. As Marcus explains, "I am very open-minded. I am willing to take in information that is difficult to accept emotionally. . . . When a market moves counter to my expectations, I have always been able to say,

'I had hoped to make a lot of money in this position, but it isn't working, so I'm getting out.'"

"The Market Was Telling Me I Was Wrong"

In April 2009, in the aftermath of the financial collapse of late 2008 and early 2009, Colm O'Shea was still very pessimistic about the markets and positioned accordingly. "But," says O'Shea, "the market was telling me I was wrong." O'Shea described his thought process at the time: "China is turning around, metal prices are turning higher, and the Australian dollar is moving up. What is that telling me? There is a recovery somewhere in the world. . . . So I can't stick with the-whole-world-is-terrible thesis. What hypothesis would fit the actual developments? Asia actually looks all right now. A scenario that would fit is an Asian-led recovery."

Recognizing that his major fundamental view was wrong, O'Shea abandoned it. Sticking with his original market expectations would have been disastrous, as both equity and commodity markets embarked on a multiyear rally. Instead, by having the flexibility to recognize his worldview was wrong and reversing his market directional bias, O'Shea achieved a profitable year, even though his original market outlook was totally incorrect.

O'Shea cites George Soros as a paragon of flexibility. "George Soros," he says, "has the least regret of anyone I have ever met. . . . He has no emotional attachment to an idea. When a trade is wrong, he will just cut it, move on, and do something else. I remember one time he had this huge FX [foreign exchange] position. He made something like $250 million on it in one day. He was quoted in the financial press talking about the position. It sounded like a major strategic view he had. Then the market went the other way, and the position just disappeared. It was gone."

Jones Reverses Course

I interviewed Paul Tudor Jones on separate visits spaced about two weeks apart. On the first interview Jones was very bearish on the stock market and heavily short the Standard & Poor's (S&P) 500 index. By my second visit, his view on the stock market had changed dramatically. The failure of the stock market to follow through on the downside as he had anticipated convinced Jones that he was wrong. "This market is sold out," he announced emphatically on my second visit. He not only had abandoned his original short position but had gone long based on the evidence that his original projection was wrong. This 180-degree shift within a short time span exemplified the extreme flexibility that underlies Jones's trading success. And, yes, his change of heart proved well timed, as the market moved sharply higher in the ensuing weeks.

Caught by a Surprise

At a time when Michael Platt held a massive long position in European interest rate futures, the European Central Bank (ECB) hiked rates very unexpectedly. It was a devastating hit for the position, but Platt was completely unaware of the situation because, at the time, he was on a flight from London to South Africa. As soon as his plane landed, he received an urgent call from his assistant, telling him what had happened and asking for instructions.

"How much are we down?" asked Platt.

"About $70 million to $80 million," his assistant replied.

Platt reasoned that if the ECB had started raising rates, the rate hikes were likely to continue. He could see the trade turning into a $250 million loss within a week if he didn't act quickly. "Dump everything!" he instructed his assistant.

When I am wrong, the only instinct I have
is to get out. If I was thinking one way,
and now I can see that it was a real mistake,
then I am probably not the only person
in shock, so I'd better be the first one
to sell. I don't care what the price is.

Michael Platt

Commenting on this experience, Platt said, "When I am wrong, the only instinct I have is to get out. If I was thinking one way, and now I can see that it was a real mistake, then I am probably not the only person in shock, so I'd better be the first one to sell. I don't care what the price is."

Surviving the Worst Trading Blunder Ever

Perhaps the best example I ever came across of lack of loyalty to a position involved Stanley Druckenmiller, whose Duquesne Capital Management hedge fund achieved an average annual return near 30 percent over a 25-year period—surely one of the best long-term track records ever. Our story begins on October 16, 1987. If you are having trouble placing the significance of that date, I'll give you a hint—it was a Friday.

At the time, Druckenmiller was managing multiple funds for Dreyfus in addition to his own Duquesne fund. Druckenmiller came into that Friday net short. Many people forget that the October 19, 1987 crash was not an abrupt event that materialized out of nowhere. Prior to that day, the market was, in fact, in the midst of a near 20 percent slide that had begun two months earlier, with 9 percent of the decline occurring in the prior week alone. By the afternoon of Friday, October 16, 1987, Druckenmiller decided the market had fallen far enough and was near what he believed would be a major support area. So he covered his short position. Bad move, right? Well, it was actually much worse. He not only covered his short position, but also went net long—heavily long. In fact, on that day, Druckenmiller switched from net short to 130 percent long (that is, a leveraged long position).

In the past, when describing this episode in a talk, I used to ask the audience if anyone had ever made a worse trading mistake. I stopped asking the question because I realized you couldn't even make up a worse trading blunder than switching from a net short equity position on Friday, October 16, 1987 to a leveraged long position.

Despite this enormous error, if you check Druckenmiller's track record, incredibly, October 1987 shows up as only a moderate loss. How is that possible? Well, first of all, during the first half of the month, Druckenmiller was short, so he made money. Now here is the thing: Between Friday's close and Monday's opening, Druckenmiller decided he had made a terrible mistake. Why is not important here. If you are curious, the reasons were fully detailed in *The New Market Wizards*. What is important is that Druckenmiller realized he had gravely erred by going heavily long and was determined to get out of his position Monday morning. The only problem with this plan was that the market opened enormously lower on Monday morning. So what did Druckenmiller do? He covered his entire new long position in the first hour of trading on Monday. Not only did he cover his long position, he went net short again! Think of the incredible lack of loyalty to a position that is required to reverse a large position and then reverse it again on the next trading day after the market had moved tremendously against the previously reversed position.

Good traders liquidate their positions when they believe they are wrong; great traders reverse their positions when they believe they are wrong.

Good traders liquidate their positions when they believe they are wrong; great traders reverse their positions when they believe they are wrong. If you want to succeed as a trader, you can't have loyalty to your position.

A Bad Idea Transformed

Flexibility, or lack of loyalty, also applies to entering trades, as illustrated by Jamie Mai's biggest short trade in 2011. Jamie Mai is the portfolio manager of Cornwall Capital, a hedge fund with strong return/risk numbers, which was one of big winners on the short side of subprime mortgage-backed securities that was originally profiled in Michael Lewis's excellent book, *The Big Short*. Indeed, it was Lewis's book that made me aware of Mai and led to my interviewing him for *Hedge Fund Market Wizards*.

In 2011, Mai noted that China, which was both the world's largest producer and its largest consumer of coal, had transitioned from being a net exporter to a net importer and that this trend was accelerating. It had taken a decade for Chinese coal exports to decline from 100 million tons to zero, but only two years for imports to grow by one-and-a-half times this amount. Mai's initial impression was that this huge, unabated growth in Chinese coal imports would lead to a sharp increase in demand for dry bulk freight. Moreover, the dry bulk shippers were trading at depressed cash flow multiples. Going long these stocks seemed like a perfect trade. But Mai, who comes from a private equity background, is very deliberate in his trade placement; every trade idea must be thoroughly researched before it is implemented. As Mai dug deeper, he discovered that high freight rates due to rising commodity demand from emerging market economies had led to a shipbuilding boom several years earlier and that these freighters were just coming onstream, with fleet capacity increases running at about 20 percent annually. Mai realized that even with the most optimistic expectations for freighter demand by China, there was still going to be a large surplus of dry bulk capacity coming on line. So, ironically, although Mai had started out with the idea of going long dry bulk shippers, he ended up doing the reverse trade by going short via long out-of-the-money put positions—the firm's highest-conviction short trade for the year.

Don't Publicize Your Market Calls

As a tangential comment, you should be very wary of trumpeting your predictions about what a market will do. Why? Because if you announce what you believe a market will do, presumably to impress others with your market acumen, you will tend to become invested in that prediction. If the evolving price action and market facts seem to contradict your forecast, you will be more reluctant to change your view than you might otherwise have been. You will find all sorts of reasons why your original forecast might still be right. Paul Tudor Jones is very cognizant of the danger of letting prior market pronouncements affect trading, an issue he specifically addressed. "I avoid letting my trading opinions be influenced by comments I may have made on the record about a market."

In his early trading years, Ed Seykota had fallen into the trap of broadcasting his opinions. He told a lot of friends that he expected silver prices to keep going up. Then, when silver went down instead, he kept ignoring all the market signs that he was wrong and told himself it was just a temporary correction. "I couldn't afford to be wrong," said Seykota, recalling this episode. Fortunately, he was saved by his subconscious. He kept having dreams in which a big, silver aircraft started going down, headed for an inevitable crash. Seykota got the message. "I eventually dumped my silver position," said Seykota. "I even went short, and the dreams stopped."

Chapter Fifteen

Size Matters

The Power of Bet Size

Edward Thorp's track record must certainly stand as one of the best of all time. His original fund, Princeton Newport Partners, achieved an annualized gross return of 19.1 percent (15.1 percent after fees) over a 19-year period. Even more impressive was the extraordinary consistency of return: 227 out of 230 winning months and a worst monthly loss under 1 percent. A second fund, Ridgeline Partners, averaged 21 percent annually over a 10-year period with only a 7 percent annualized volatility.

Before he ever became interested in markets, Edward Thorp was a math professor whose avocation was devising methods to win at various casino games—an endeavor widely assumed to be impossible. After all, how could anyone possibly devise a winning strategy for games in which the player had a negative edge? One might think that a math professor would be the last person to devote time to such a seemingly futile goal. Thorp, however, approached the problem in a completely unconventional manner. For example, in roulette, Thorpe, along with Claude Shannon (known as "the father of information theory"), created a miniature computer that used Newtonian physics to predict the octant of the wheel in which the ball was most likely to land.

***

By analogy to blackjack, trading larger for higher-probability trades and smaller, or not at all, for lower-probability trades could even transform a losing strategy into a winning one.

In blackjack, Thorp's insight was that by betting more on high-probability hands than on low-probability hands, it was possible to transform a game with a negative edge into a game with a positive edge. This insight has important ramifications for trading: varying position size could improve performance. By analogy to blackjack, trading larger for higher-probability trades and smaller, or not at all, for lower-probability trades could even transform a losing strategy into a winning one. Although probabilities cannot be accurately defined in trading as they are in blackjack, traders can often still differentiate between higher- and lower-probability trades. For example, if a trader does better on high-confidence trades, then the degree of confidence can serve as a proxy for the probability of winning. The implication then is that instead of risking an equal amount on each trade, more risk should be allocated to higher-confidence trades and less to lower-confidence trades.

Michael Marcus specifically cited varying position size as a key element of his success. He recognized that he did much better on trades when the fundamentals, the chart pattern, and the market tone (how the market responded to news) all were supportive to the trade. He realized that he would probably be better off if he restricted his trading to only those trades that met all three conditions. However, such opportunities didn't occur that often, and by his own admission, he "enjoyed the game too much" to wait patiently for only those situations. "I placed the fun of the action ahead of my own criteria," he said, acknowledging that these nonoptimal trades might have been detrimental on balance. "However, the thing that saved me," Marcus said, "was that when a trade met all my criteria, I would enter five to six times the position size I was doing on the other trades."

The Danger of Size

In Paul Tudor Jones's early years in the markets when he was still a broker, he experienced the most devastating trade of his career. At the time, he was managing speculative accounts in the cotton market. The nearby July contract had been in a trading range and Jones had built up a 400-contract long position for his accounts. One day, he was on the floor of the exchange when July cotton broke below the low end of its range, but then rebounded. Jones thought that with the stops below the range having been taken out, the market would rally. In an act of bravado, he instructed his floor broker to bid higher for 100 contracts, which at the time was a very large order. In an instant, the broker for the firm that held most of the deliverable cotton stocks yelled, "Sold!" Jones immediately realized that the firm intended to deliver its stocks against the July contract he held and that the 400-point premium of July over the following contract (October) price was going to quickly evaporate. He knew right then that he was on the wrong side of the market and instructed his floor broker to sell as much as he could. The market plunged and within 60 seconds was locked limit down. He had only been able to liquidate less than half of his position.

The next morning, the market locked limit down again before Jones could fully liquidate his remaining position.

Finally, on the following day, he was able to get out of the remainder of his position, selling some contracts as much as 400 points below the point he had known he wanted to be out.

Jones said that his problem was not the number of points he lost on the trade, but rather that he was trading far too many contracts relative to the equity he managed. His accounts lost about 60 to 70 percent on that single trade! Recalling this painful experience, Jones said, "I was totally demoralized. I said, 'I am not cut out for this business; I don't think I can hack it much longer.' I was so depressed that I nearly quit. . . . It was at that point that I said, 'Mr. Stupid, why risk everything on one trade? Why not make your life a pursuit of happiness rather than pain?'"

That trade was so traumatic that it changed Jones. His focus shifted to what he could lose on a trade, not what he could make. He became much more defensive in his trading. He would never again take a huge risk on a single trade.

Overtrading was also inherent in a disastrous trade that caused Bruce Kovner to lose half of his accumulated profits in a single day. This trade, which is detailed in Chapter 17, instilled in him a bias for maintaining smaller positions. Kovner believes most novice traders trade too large. His advice to traders is: "Undertrade, undertrade, undertrade. . . . Whatever you think your position ought to be, cut it at least in half. My experience with novice traders is that they trade three to five times too big. They are taking 5 to 10 percent risks on a trade when they should be taking 1 to 2 percent risks."

In our interview, Kovner mentioned that he had tried to train about 30 traders, but that only about five of them turned out to be good traders. I asked him if there was some distinguishing characteristic between the majority who weren't successful at trading versus the minority who were. One of the key differences Kovner highlighted was that the successful traders were disciplined in sizing their positions correctly. "A greedy trader always blows up," he said.

—————————————— ∽ ——————————————

The larger the position, the greater the danger that trading decisions will be driven by fear rather than by judgment and experience.

The larger the position, the greater the danger that trading decisions will be driven by fear rather than by judgment and experience. Steve Clark, the portfolio manager for the London-based Omni Global Fund,[1] a strategy with a strong return/risk record, said that you have to trade within your "emotional capacity." Otherwise, you will be prone to getting out of good trades on meaningless corrections and losing money on trades that would have been winners. According to Clark, one sure way of knowing your position is too large is if you wake up worrying about it.

Howard Seidler, one of the best-performing of the group of traders trained by Richard Dennis and William Eckhardt, popularly known as the Turtles, learned the lesson of trading beyond his "emotional capacity" very early in his trading career. After he had taken a short position, the market started moving in his direction so he decided to double the position. Shortly afterward, the market started moving back up. It wasn't a large move, but because of the doubled position size, Seidler was so concerned about his losses that he liquidated not only his added position, but his original position as well. Two days later, the market collapsed as he had originally anticipated. If Seidler had just maintained his original position, he would have made a large profit on the trade, but because he had traded too large and then overreacted, he missed the entire profit opportunity. Speaking of this experience, Seidler said, "There are certain lessons that you absolutely have to learn to be a successful trader. One of those lessons is that you can't win if you're trading at a leverage size that makes you fearful of the market."

Marty Schwartz cautioned traders against increasing their size too quickly when they started to make money. "Most people make the mistake of increasing their bets as soon as they start making money," he said. "That is a quick way to get wiped out." He advised waiting until you had at least doubled your capital before beginning to trade larger.

Stepping on the Accelerator

Although trading too large is one of the most common reasons why traders fail, there are times when trading large is justified, and even desirable. Stanley Druckenmiller said that one of the most important lessons he learned from George Soros was that "it's not whether you're right or wrong that's important, but how much money you make when you're right and how much you lose when you're wrong." He said that the few times Soros ever criticized him was when he was right on the market but didn't "maximize the opportunity." As an example, Druckenmiller cited an episode that occurred shortly after he started working for Soros. At the time, Druckenmiller was very bearish on the dollar versus the deutsche mark and had placed what he thought was a large position. The position had started working in his favor, and Druckenmiller felt rather proud of himself. Soros came into Druckenmiller's office and they talked about the trade.

"How big a position do you have?" asked Soros.

"One billion dollars," answered Druckenmiller.

"You call that a position?" said Soros dismissively. Soros encouraged Druckenmiller to double the position, which he did, and the trade went dramatically further in his favor.

Druckenmiller says that Soros taught him that "when you have tremendous conviction on a trade, you have to go for the jugular. It takes courage to be a pig."

Although Druckenmiller had not yet joined Soros Management at the time, he heard what had happened at the firm in the aftermath of the Plaza Accord in 1985, a meeting in which the United States, United Kingdom, West Germany, France, and Japan agreed to a unified policy to depreciate the dollar versus the other currencies. Soros had been heavily long the yen going into the meeting, and other traders in the office had piggybacked his position. The Monday morning after the agreement had been reached, the yen opened 800 points higher. The traders at Soros Management couldn't believe the size of their sudden windfall gain and started taking profits. Soros came bolting out of the door, telling them to stop selling the yen and that he would assume their positions. Druckenmiller drew the lesson from this episode. "While these other traders were congratulating themselves for having taken the biggest profit in their lives, Soros was looking at the big picture. The government had just told him that the dollar was going to go down for the next year, so why shouldn't he be a pig and buy more [yen]?"

Readers should be careful in the lesson they draw from this section. The point is not that traders should be willing to take large, aggressive trades, but rather that they should be willing take larger trades *when they have very high conviction*.

Volatility and Trading Size

Too many traders maintain the same position sizing through different market conditions. However, if the desire is to keep risk approximately equal through time, then position sizing needs to adjust for significant changes in market volatility. Colm O'Shea recalls that in 2008 he would run across managers who said they had cut their risk in half. O'Shea would say, "Half—that's quite a lot." Then they would continue and say, "Yes, my leverage was four, and it is now two." O'Shea would answer, "Do you realize volatility has gone up five times?" These managers had thought they had reduced risk, but in volatility-adjusted terms, their risk had actually gone up.

Correlation and Trading Size

Different positions are not independent like separate coin tosses. Although they sometimes may be independent, at other times they may be significantly correlated. If different positions are positively correlated, then the probability of a portfolio loss of any given magnitude is increased because there will be a tendency for losses in different positions to occur simultaneously. To account for this greater risk, position sizing should be reduced when different positions are positively correlated.

After a long career of trading a variety of arbitrage strategies, Edward Thorp developed and traded a trend-following strategy. When I asked him how he achieved significantly better return/risk performance than other trend-following practitioners, he attributed the improvement, in part, to incorporating a risk-reduction strategy based on correlations. He described the process as follows: "We traded a correlation matrix that was used to reduce exposures in correlated markets. If two markets were highly correlated and the technical system went long one and short the other, that was great. But if it wanted to go long both or short both, we would take a smaller position in each."

Chapter Sixteen

Doing the Uncomfortable Thing

The Outperforming Monkey

William Eckhardt believes that the natural human tendency to seek comfort leads people to make decisions that are worse than random in trading. I want to be clear. You have probably heard the famous quote by Burton Malkiel, "A blindfolded monkey throwing darts at a newspaper's financial pages could select a portfolio that would do just as well as one carefully selected by experts," or some variation of that theme frequently uttered by those deriding the purported folly of trying to beat the market. Eckhardt is not saying that. He is not saying a monkey could do as well as the professional money managers. Eckhardt is saying the monkey will do *better*.

What feels good is often the wrong thing to do.

William Eckhardt

Now, why will the monkey do better? The monkey will do better because humans have evolved to seek comfort, and the markets don't pay off for being comfortable. In the markets, seeking comfort means doing what is emotionally satisfying. Eckhardt says, "What feels good is often the wrong thing to do." He quotes his former trading partner, Richard Dennis, who used to say, "If it feels good, don't do it."

As an example of doing what feels good in the markets, Eckhardt cites what he terms "the call of the countertrend." Buying on weakness and selling on strength appeals to the natural human desire to buy cheap and sell dear. If you buy a stock when it falls to a six-month low, it feels good because you are smarter than everyone else who bought that stock in the past six months. Although these trades may feel better at the moment of implementation, for most people, following such a countertrend approach will be a losing, and possibly even disastrous, strategy.

As another example, Eckhardt explains that because most small profits tend to vanish, people learn the lesson to cash in profits right away, which may feel good, but is detrimental over the long run because it will also impede the ability earn large profits on any trade. As a third example, Eckhardt says that the tendency of markets to trade through the same price repeatedly leads people to hold on to bad trades in the hope that if they wait long enough, the market will return to their entry level.

In all these cases, the action that feels good—getting a bargain, locking in a profit, holding out hope for avoiding a loss—is usually the wrong thing to do. The need for emotional satisfaction will lead most people to make decisions that are even worse than random, which is why the dart-throwing monkey will do better.

As an empirical demonstration of how most people's biases will lead them to make decisions that are worse than random, Eckhardt told the story of how one of Richard Dennis's employees entered a charting contest that required predicting the year-end prices for a number of markets. This employee simply used the current prices of all the markets for his predictions. He finished in the top five among hundreds of contestants. In other words, at least 95 percent, and probably closer to 99 percent, of all the entrants' predictions were worse than random.

The Inadvertent Experiment

In his book *The Little Book That Beats the Market*, Joel Greenblatt provided a value-based indicator for ranking stocks. He called this ranking indicator the Magic Formula, a name that poked fun at the hype normally accompanying market indicators, but also referred to the surprising efficacy of the measure. In fact, Greenblatt and his trading partner, Rob Goldstein, were so impressed with how well the Magic Formula worked that they set up an eponymous website that investors could use to pick their own stocks from a limited list of equities selected based on the value rankings of the formula. Investors were encouraged to pick at least 20 to 30 stocks from the list to get close to the average performance of these stocks, as opposed to being overly dependent on a few names. As a last-minute addition, they also included a check box that gave investors the option of having their account managed rather than picking the stocks themselves. It turned out that less 10 percent of people using the site for investment chose to do their own selection—the original concept—while the overwhelming majority chose the managed portfolio option.

Greenblatt then tracked how the self-managed portfolios fared versus the managed portfolios. After the first two years, on average, the managed portfolios outperformed the self-managed portfolios by 25 percent, *even though both were constructed from the same list of stocks.* The differential between the managed and the self-managed portfolios reflected the impact of human selection and timing decisions. Letting investors make their own decisions (picking specific stocks from the list and timing the purchase and sale of these stocks) destroyed all the performance vis-à-vis investing equal-dollar amounts in a diversified portfolio of these stocks without any attempt to time the entries and exits of the holdings.

∼

**[Investors] did much worse than random
in selecting stocks from our prescreened list,
probably because by avoiding the stocks
that were particularly painful to own,
they missed some of the biggest winners.**

Joel Greenblatt

I asked Greenblatt why he thought the investors making their own decisions did so much worse. Greenblatt replied, "They took their exposure down when the market fell. They tended to sell when individual stocks or their portfolio as a whole underperformed. They did much worse than random in selecting stocks from our prescreened list, probably because by avoiding the stocks that were particularly painful to own, they missed some of the biggest winners." Think about it. Don't these sound like decisions made to seek comfort?

Greenblatt had inadvertently created a control group experiment that demonstrated the impact of human decisions in the market vis-à-vis a well-defined benchmark—a diversified portfolio consisting of the same list of stocks without any selection or timing inputs. Investors could have achieved the same expected return (with sampling variation) if they had *randomly* selected their stocks, investing *equal-dollar* amounts in each, and applying the same *timing-free* buy-and-hold approach. Or, equivalently, the same expected return could have been achieved from a portfolio based on the dart throws of a monkey at the list of the selected stocks. Greenblatt's inadvertent experiment effectively provided a real-life validation of Eckhardt's contention that the proverbial monkey would outperform humans making their own investment decisions.

Behavioral Economics and Trading

Eckhardt ties in human biases to the tendency for the majority of market participants to lose. As Eckhardt explains it, "There is a persistent overall tendency for equity to flow from the many to the few. In the long run, the majority loses.

The implication for the trader is that to win you have to act like the minority. If you bring normal human habits and tendencies to trading, you'll gravitate toward the majority and invariably lose."

Eckhardt's observations are well aligned with the findings of behavioral economists whose research has demonstrated that people inherently make irrational investment decisions. For example, in one classic experiment conducted by Daniel Kahneman and Amos Tversky, pioneers in the field of prospect theory, subjects were given a hypothetical choice between a sure $3,000 gain versus an 80 percent chance of a $4,000 gain and a 20 percent chance of not getting anything.[1] The vast majority of people preferred the sure $3,000 gain, even though the other alternative had a higher expected gain ($0.80 \times \$4,000 = \$3,200$). Then they flipped the question around and gave people a choice between a certain loss of $3,000 versus an 80 percent chance of losing $4,000 and a 20 percent chance of not losing anything. In this case, the vast majority chose to gamble and take the 80 percent chance of a $4,000 loss, even though the expected loss would be $3,200. In both cases, people made irrational choices because they selected the alternative with the smaller expected gain or larger expected loss. Why? Because the experiment reflects a quirk in human behavior in regard to risk and gain: People are risk averse when it comes to gains, but are risk takers when it comes to avoiding a loss.

This behavioral quirk relates very much to trading, as it explains why people tend to let their losses run and cut their profits short. So the old cliché (but not any less valid advice) to "let your profits run and cut your losses short" is actually the exact opposite of what most people tend to do.[2]

Why Emotions Affect Even Computerized Trading

Interestingly, the need for emotional comfort will even have a detrimental impact on systematic trading (i.e., computerized, rule-driven trading), an area of trading one might reasonably have assumed would be free of emotionally based decisions. Typically, when people approach systematic trading, they will test their system rules and then discover that there are many past instances when following the system rules would have led to uncomfortably large equity drawdowns—an observation that will be true even if the system is profitable over the long run. The natural instinct is to revise the system rules or add additional rules that mitigate these poorly performing past periods. This process can be repeated multiple times, making the simulated equity curve smoother and smoother with each iteration. In effect, the natural inclination is to optimize system rules for past price behavior. The resulting final optimized system will generate an equity curve that looks like a money machine. Such a highly optimized system will be much more comfortable to trade because, after all, look how well it would have done in the past.

The irony, however, is that the more a system has been optimized to improve its past performance, the less likely it is to perform well in the future. The rub is that the system's impressive simulated results are achieved with the hindsight knowledge of past prices. Future prices will be different, so the more the system rules are tweaked to fit historical prices, the less likely the system will work on future prices. Once again, the human instinct to seek emotional comfort has negative consequences in trading—even in computerized trading!

Conclusion

The lesson of this chapter is that most people lose money in trading not only because they lack skill (that is, they don't have an edge), but also because their inclination to make the comfortable choices in trading (or investing) will actually lead to worse-than-random results. Awareness of this inherent human handicap to trading is the first step in resisting the temptation to make trading decisions that feel good but are wrong on balance.

Chapter Seventeen

Emotions
and Trading

~

F REE SOLO CLIMBING IS a sport that defies belief. The free solo climber forgoes all protective equipment in making ascents. Picture an unroped climber 2,000 feet up on a sheer, vertical rock wall, and you get the idea. Any mistake is potentially fatal. You would think that any practitioner engaged in this sport would be flooded with adrenaline—and you would be wrong.

Alex Honnold is widely acknowledged to be the best free-soloing climber in the world, whose extraordinary feats include the first free solo climb up the northwest face of Half

Dome, a 2,000-foot vertical wall in Yosemite National Park. He was featured in a segment of the October 10, 2011, episode of *60 Minutes*.

At one point, the correspondent, Lara Logan, asked Honnold, "Do you feel the adrenaline at all?"

If I get a rush, it means that something has gone horribly wrong.

Alex Honnold

Honnold replied, "There is no adrenaline rush. . . . If I get a rush, it means that something has gone horribly wrong. . . . The whole thing should be pretty slow and controlled."

Those words could just as well apply to the expert trader. The Hollywood image of trading as an adrenaline-filled, high-risk-assuming endeavor may make for good visuals, but it has nothing to do with successful trading.

Expensive Excitement

Larry Hite was once playing tennis with a friend who had gone broke trading futures. His friend couldn't understand how Larry could just follow a computerized system.

"Larry," he asked, "how can you trade the way you do? Isn't it boring?

Hite replied, "I don't trade for excitement; I trade to win."

Charles Faulkner, who has used his research on modeling human excellence to coach traders, told me about one of his early clients who was a very emotional trader. This client had developed a successful system but couldn't follow it. Faulkner taught him some techniques for emotionally detaching himself from the markets. Initially, the techniques worked, and the trader was profitable as he followed the system. One day when Faulkner was working with him, the trader was up $7,000 in the first few hours. Just as Faulkner was feeling rather smug about his apparent success in helping this trader, the trader turned to him and in a monotone said, "This is boring." The trader eventually blew up. "He knew how to go into an emotionally detached state, but he didn't like to be there," said Faulkner. The lesson is that the markets are an expensive place to look for excitement.

You Can't Win If You Have to Win

When Stanley Druckenmiller started his money management firm, Duquesne Capital Management, in 1981, he was entirely dependent on the income stream from a consulting contract with Drysdale Securities that paid him $10,000 per month. In May 1982, Drysdale Securities abruptly went out of business. As a result, Druckenmiller had a cash flow problem. His $7 million in assets under management at the time paid

$70,000 per year in fees, but his overhead was $180,000 per year. The firm's capital on hand was only $50,000. Without the consulting income from Drysdale, the survival of his management firm was threatened.

At the time, Druckenmiller was absolutely convinced that interest rates, which had receded from all-time-record highs a year earlier, would continue to decline. Druckenmiller took the firm's entire $50,000 and used it to margin a highly leveraged long position in Treasury bill futures.[1] He literally bet the company on the trade. In four days, Druckenmiller lost everything when interest rates began rising. The irony is that only one week later, rates hit their high for the cycle and never again remotely approached that level. Druckenmiller had bought T-bill futures within one week of a major bottom—you can't time a position much better than that—and still lost all his money. Druckenmiller's analysis was absolutely right, but the emotionalism that underlay the trade—excessive leverage and lack of planning in a Hail Mary attempt to save his firm—doomed it to failure. The market will seldom reward the carelessness of trades born of desperation.

Impulsive Trades

Impulsive trades can be dangerous. When asked to recall their most painful trades, the Market Wizards often cited impulsive trades as examples.

The trade that Bruce Kovner considers "far and away" his most painful trade and, psychologically, his "going-bust trade" was the product of an impulsive decision. Very early in his trading career, in 1977, there was a shortage of soybeans. Given the tight supplies and persistent strong demand, Kovner anticipated there would be fears of running out of soybeans before new crop supplies became available. To profit from this situation, Kovner put on a highly leveraged spread position, going long the old crop July contract and short the new crop November contract. His expectation was that the shortage would cause the old crop July contract to rise much more steeply than the new crop November contract. Kovner's projection was not merely right, but spectacularly right. At one point, the market entered a string of limit-up moves led by the old crop contracts. Kovner's profits were soaring.

One morning when the market reached new highs, Kovner received a call from his broker. "Soybeans are going to the moon!" his broker excitedly told him. "It looks like July is going limit up, and November is sure to follow. You are a fool to stay short the November contracts. Let me lift your November shorts for you, and when the market goes limit up for the next few days, you will make more money." Kovner agreed to cover his short November position, leaving himself just outright long the July contract.

I asked Kovner if this was a spur-of-the-moment decision. "It was a moment of insanity," he replied.

Just 15 minutes later, Kovner's broker called again. This time around, he was frantic. "I don't know how to tell you this, but the market is limit down! I don't know if I can get you out."

Kovner went into shock. He yelled at his broker to get him out of the July contract. Fortunately, the market traded off the limit for a few minutes and he was able to get out. In the following days, the market went down as quickly as it had risen. If he had not gotten out immediately, Kovner could have lost more than all his money because he was heavily margined. As it was, between the moment he agreed to let his broker liquidate only the short side of his spread position and the point when the long side was liquidated later that day, his account equity was halved.

Kovner recognized that his impulsive decision to lift the short side of his spread position in the midst of a market panic showed a complete disregard for risk. "I think what bothered me so much," Kovner said, "was the realization that I had lost a process of rationality that I thought I had."

Ironically, one of the trades that Michael Marcus recalled as being among his most painful also involved an impulsive decision made in the soybean market. Marcus went long soybeans in the great bull market of 1973, which saw soybean prices triple their previous record highs. As the rally developed, Marcus impulsively took profits on his entire position. As he described it, "I was trying to be fancy instead of staying with the trend." Ed Seykota, who worked at the same firm and served as a model for Marcus, stayed with his position, since there was no sign of a trend reversal. The soybean market then proceeded to go limit up for 12 consecutive days. During this period, Marcus dreaded going to work, knowing that soybeans would be bid limit up again and that he was out of his position while Seykota was still in his. The experience was so agonizing that one day when Marcus felt he couldn't stand it anymore, he took Thorazine to dull the pain.

Marty Schwartz warned against the danger of acting impulsively to recover trading losses. "Whenever you are hit," Schwartz said, "you are very upset emotionally. Most traders try to make it back immediately; they try to play bigger. Whenever you try to get all your losses back at once, you are most often doomed to fail."

Based on my own personal experience, I would say there is probably no class of trades with a higher failure rate than impulsive trades. Regardless of what approach you use, once you have defined a trading strategy, you should stick with the game plan and avoid impulsive trading decisions. Some examples of impulsive trading decisions are putting on an unplanned trade, taking profits on a position before either the target objective or the stop loss is reached, and implementing a trade because a friend or some so-called market expert recommended it.

Don't Confuse Intuition with Impulse

Impulsive trades should not be confused with intuitive trades. The former are almost invariably bad ideas, while the latter can be high-probability trades for experienced traders.

There is nothing mystical or superstitious about intuition. As I see it, intuition is simply subconscious experience. When a trader has an intuition that the market will move in a given direction, it is often a subconscious recognition of similar past situations.

∼

The trick is to differentiate between what you *want* to happen and what you *know* will happen.

A trader

Emotional influences can compromise the objectivity of market analysis and trading decisions. For example, a trader who is long will be more inclined to dismiss market evidence that she would otherwise have interpreted as bearish in the absence of a position. It may just be too painful to accept a bearish forecast when she is long and hoping for higher prices. Or a trader might ignore signs that the market is moving higher because he has procrastinated in placing the position, and entering now would confirm the mistake of not having bought previously when prices were lower. As a final example, a trader who is on the record with a forecast for the market moving higher or lower will be reluctant to accept contradictory evidence. These types of internal constraints may cloud conscious analysis and trading decisions and prevent a trader from recognizing evidence that is uncomfortable to accept. The subconscious mind, however, is not inhibited by such constraints. As one trader I interviewed (who requested anonymity) said, "The trick is to differentiate between what you *want* to happen and what you *know* will happen."

What we call "intuition" may just be the objective synthesis of the available information based on past experience, unhindered by emotional distortions. Unfortunately, we cannot tap into our subconscious thoughts at will. However, when these market views come through as intuition, the trader should pay attention.

Dynamic versus Static Trading

The Need to Adapt

Although most (and maybe all) of the trading principles discussed in this book are timeless, trading strategies and methodologies need to adapt. When I asked Colm O'Shea if there were specific trading rules he followed, he replied, "I use risk guidelines, but I don't believe in rules that way. Traders who are successful over the long run adapt. If they do use rules, and you meet them 10 years later, they will have broken those rules. Why? Because the world has changed. Rules are only applicable to a market at a specific time. Traders who fail may have great rules that work, but then stop working. They stick to the rules because the rules used to work, and they are quite annoyed that they are losing even though they are still doing what they used to do. They don't realize that the world has moved on without them."

Traders who are successful over the long run adapt.

Colm O'Shea

Edward Thorp provided a perfect example of how successful traders adapt. Among the many firsts Thorp achieved in his long career, he was the first to implement statistical arbitrage as a strategy. Statistical arbitrage is a type of market-neutral strategy in which portfolios are constructed consisting of large numbers of long and short equity positions, balanced to minimize market directional moves and other risks. The strategy will go long underpriced equities and short overpriced equities, dynamically adjusting the holdings as prices change. Typically, but not necessarily always, a mean-reversion strategy will be used to determine which stocks are underpriced and which are overpriced.

In 1979, Thorp launched a research effort he called the "indicators project." He looked for indicators that might have some predictive value for individual equity prices. Thorp and his team examined a broad range of possible indicators, including earnings surprises, dividend payout rates, book-to-price ratios, and so on. As part of this project, one of the researchers looked at the stocks that had been up and down the most in the recent past. This factor turned out to be by far the most effective indicator tested in predicting near-term equity prices. Essentially, the stocks that were up the most tended to underperform in the subsequent period, while the stocks that were down the most tended to outperform. They called their strategy MUD for most up, most down.

In the initial incarnation of the strategy, Thorp sought to control risk by balancing the long and short equity exposures. The strategy worked very well with reasonable risk control, but eventually the return/risk performance started to deteriorate. At this point, Thorp revised the strategy by constructing portfolios that were not only market neutral but also sector neutral. Then when even the sector-neutral model showed signs of losing its edge, Thorp switched to a strategy that neutralized the portfolio to various mathematically defined factors. By the time this third iteration was adopted, the original system version had significantly degraded. By continually adapting the strategy as needed, Thorp was able to maintain superior return/risk performance, whereas if he had stayed with the original system that had worked so well at one time, the profitability would have eventually evaporated.

Scaling versus Single-Price Entry and Exit

You don't have to get into or out of a position all at once. Most traders tend to pick a single entry price and a single exit price. It is often better to scale into and out of positions. For example, consider a common dilemma faced by traders. Let's say you have a strong conviction that a market will move higher, but prices have just witnessed a significant upswing. You are concerned that if you buy now and there is a correction, the initial loss may force you out of the market, even if you are right about the long-term direction. On the other hand, if the trade is really good, there is a substantial chance that waiting for a pullback will result in missing the entire move. There is a third alternative, however: You can buy a partial position at the market and then seek to enter the remainder of the position using a scale-down entry process. This scale-down buying approach will ensure that you have at least a partial position if the market keeps going, without assuming the implicit risk of buying the entire position after a substantial advance. By reducing the average entry price, it will also mitigate the chances of abandoning a good long-term trade because of an initial loss from entry.

An analogous perspective would also apply to getting out of a position. For example, assume you are in a long position with a large gain and are concerned about surrendering those profits. If you get out of the entire position and the advance continues, you can miss out on a substantial portion of the total move. If, however, you hold on to the entire position and the market reverses, you can end up giving back a large portion of the gain. As an alternative, scaling out of the position will ensure that you still have a partial position if the move continues, while mitigating a surrender of profits if the market reverses. Bill Lipschutz, a former head of global foreign exchange (FX) trading at Salomon Brothers and the portfolio manager for Hathersage Capital Management, an FX money management firm, attributed his ability to stay with good long-term trades to his use of scaling-out orders: "It has enabled me to stay with long-term winners much longer than I've seen most traders stay with their positions."

Avoid the temptation of wanting to be completely right. By shunning all-or-nothing decisions and instead scaling in and scaling out of positions, you will never get the best outcome, but you will never get the worst one, either.

Trading around Positions

Most traders tend to view trades as a two-step process: a decision when (or where) to enter and a decision when (or where) to exit. It may be better to view trading as a dynamic process between entry and exit points rather than a static one.

Perhaps no one I ever interviewed exemplified a dynamic trading process more than Jimmy Balodimas, a very successful proprietary trader for First New York Securities. He is the epitome of an unorthodox trader. I started my chapter on Balodimas in *Hedge Fund Market Wizards* with the sentence "Jimmy Balodimas breaks all the rules." And he does. He will sell into sharp rallies and buy into plunging markets. He will add to losers and cut winners short. I don't advise anyone to try to copy Balodimas's trading method, which I think would be financial suicide for most people. But there is one element—and only one element—of his trading style that I think can be beneficial to many traders. This particular aspect of his trading, which we will get to soon, explains how Balodimas can often be net profitable, even when he is on the wrong side of the market.

I first interviewed Balodimas on February 22, 2011, a day when the stock market was down sharply. Prior to that day, the month had been particularly brutal for shorts, as the market reached new highs almost daily, never taking more than three days to do so. Balodimas had been heavily short throughout February. The steep sell-off on the 22nd surrendered a little less than half of the month's gain, but it was enough for Balodimas to recover more than his entire loss for the month to date.

One of the first questions I asked Balodimas was: "How can you still be ahead when you have been on the wrong side of the market?"

I always take some money off the table when the market is in my favor. . . . That saves me a lot of money, because when the market rallies, I have a smaller position.

Jimmy Balodimas

He answered, speaking from his perspective as a short at the time of our interview, "I always take some money off the table when the market is in my favor. . . . That saves me a lot of money, because when the market rallies, I have a smaller position. That is a habit I have had since day one. I always take money off the table when it's in my favor. Always, always, always."

The adjustment of position size counter to market fluctuations (e.g., reducing a short position on a break and rebuilding to a full position on a rally) is a key element in Balodimas's success. He is so skillful in trading around his positions that he is sometimes, as in this instance, net profitable even when he is on wrong side of the market trend. Although few traders will be able to match Balodimas's innate skill in trading around positions, many traders may find a dynamic rather than static approach to trades beneficial.

How might a dynamic trading approach be used in practice? The basic idea is that the position size of a trade would be reduced on a profitable move and rebuilt on a subsequent correction. Any time a position was lightened and the market retraced to the reentry point, a profit would be generated that otherwise would not have been realized. It is even possible for a trade that fails to exhibit a favorable net price change, as measured from original entry to final exit, to be profitable as a result of trading against the position (i.e., reducing exposure on favorable price swings and increasing exposure on subsequent adverse price moves).

Another important benefit of reducing exposure on a favorable price move is that it will lessen the chances of being knocked out of a good trade on a price correction, since if the position has already been reduced, a correction would have less impact and might even be deemed desirable to provide an opportunity to reenter the liquidated portion of the trade. For example, let's say you buy a stock at 40 with a target objective of 50 and an expectation of interim resistance at 45. Given these assumptions, you might use a strategy of reducing exposure at 45 and reinstating the full position on a pullback. This type of approach will make you a stronger holder on a pullback. In contrast, if a static trading approach were used instead, a pullback could lead to concerns that the entire profits on the trade might be lost, thereby increasing the chances that the trade would be fully liquidated.

The only time when a strategy of taking partial profits on favorable price moves and reinstating on corrections will be net detrimental is when the market keeps moving in the intended direction without pulling back to the reentry level. But in this instance, by definition, the retained portion of the position will be very profitable. So, on balance, this type of dynamic trading process can increase profits on price moves with corrections, as well as improve the chances of staying with good trades, at the expense of giving up a portion of profits on trades that move smoothly in the intended direction. Trading around positions will not necessarily be a good fit for all traders, but some traders should find the approach very beneficial.

Market Response

~

A COUNTER-TO-ANTICIPATED RESPONSE TO market news may be more meaningful than the news item itself. Marty Schwartz credited his friend Bob Zoellner with teaching him how to analyze market action. Schwartz summarized the basic principle: "When the market gets good news and goes down, it means the market is very weak; when it gets bad news and goes up, it means the market is healthy." Many of the traders I interviewed recalled trading experiences that echoed this theme.

――――――――――――――― ∼ ―――――――――――――――

When the market gets good news and goes down, it means the market is very weak; when it gets bad news and goes up, it means the market is healthy.

Marty Schwartz

Gold and the First Iraq War

Randy McKay described a trading approach that incorporated market response to fundamental news. Describing how he used fundamentals, McKay said, "I don't think, 'Supply is too large and the market is going down.' Rather, I watch how the market responds to fundamental information." McKay provided the classic example of the behavior of the gold market in response to the first Iraq war, the Gulf War, which began in January 1991. On the eve of the first U.S. air strike, gold was trading just below the psychologically important $400 level. During the night when U.S planes started the attack, gold rallied past the $400 level, moving to $410 in the Asian markets, but then retreated back to $390—lower than it was before the war-induced rally started. McKay viewed gold's price decline in the face of what was expected to be bullish news as a very bearish sign. The next morning, gold opened sharply lower in the U.S. market and continued to decline in the ensuing months.

McKay Gets Interested in Stocks

McKay had long been influenced by the market's response to news. Nine years earlier, in 1982, he became very bullish on the stock market. McKay was a futures trader and had never even traded stocks before. His conviction about the stock market was so strong, however, that it compelled him to open a stock account. I asked McKay what made him so convinced that the stock market was going higher when he had never even traded stocks. He answered, "Part of it was just seeing the market up almost every day without any particular supporting news. In fact, the news was actually quite negative: Inflation, interest rates, and unemployment were all still very high." Here too, market tone—the ability of stock prices to advance steadily despite ostensibly bearish fundamentals—provided the crucial price clue.

Dalio Is Surprised

Ray Dalio recalled episodes early in his career when he was surprised by the market response to news. In 1971, after graduating from college, Dalio worked as a clerk on the New York Stock Exchange. On August 15, President Richard Nixon took the United States off the gold standard, causing an upheaval in the monetary system. Dalio thought this event was bearish news, but to his surprise, the market rallied.

Eleven years later, with the United States mired in a recession and unemployment above 11 percent, Mexico defaulted on its debt. Dalio knew that the U.S. banks held large amounts of capital in Latin American debt. He naturally assumed that the default would be terrible for the stock market. Dalio's expectations could not have been more wrong. The default by Mexico was near the exact bottom of the stock market and marked the beginning of an 18-year rally.

Speaking of both these experiences where the market reaction was exactly inverse to his expectations, Dalio said, "In both the abandonment of the gold standard in 1971 and in the Mexico default in 1982, I learned that a crisis development that leads to central banks easing and coming to the rescue can swamp the impact of the crisis itself." Indeed, we witnessed another dramatic example of this observation in the major bull market that followed on the heels of the 2008-to-2009 financial meltdown—a recovery that was heavily aided by aggressive central bank intervention.

Investors are often baffled when markets respond counterintuitively to news events. This seemingly paradoxical behavior can be explained by the fact that markets often anticipate the news and discount the impending event. For example, a default in Latin American debt in 1982 was widely anticipated before Mexico actually defaulted. Ironically, the very occurrence of an anticipated event removes it as a market concern, thereby leading to a counter-to-anticipated price response. Another factor that explains bullish market action in response to bearish news is that the bearish event—especially if it is significant—can trigger bullish repercussions. For example, developments that have very negative implications for the economy and market sentiment can prompt central bank measures that lead to a rally.

A Most Bullish Report

The market does not necessarily need to witness a strong counter-to-anticipated response to fundamental news to provide a market-tone-based signal; a weak response to what was expected to be a major bullish or bearish event can have the same implications.

Always ask yourself, "How many people are left to act on this particular idea?" You have to consider whether the market has already discounted your idea.

Michael Marcus

Michael Marcus said, "Always ask yourself, 'How many people are left to act on this particular idea?' You have to consider whether the market has already discounted your idea."

"How can you possibly evaluate that?" I asked him.

Marcus explained it was a matter of reading market tone. He provided what he considered the classic example, which involved a bull market in soybeans in the late 1970s. At the time, there was a severe shortage of soybeans, and each week, the government export report would drive prices higher. One day just after the latest weekly report was released, Marcus received a call from someone at his company. The caller said, "I have good news and I have bad news."

"Okay, what is the good news?" Marcus asked.

"The good news is that the export commitment figure was fantastic. The bad news is that you don't have a limit position." (A limit position is the maximum permissible speculative position size.)

The report was so bullish that the general expectations were that the market would be limit up for three consecutive days. Even though he was heavily long, and the report implied his position would realize spectacular profits, Marcus actually felt a little depressed because he did not have the maximum permissible position for a speculator. The next morning, Marcus put in an order to buy more contracts on the opening, just in case he got lucky and the market traded momentarily before locking limit up. Then, "I sat back to watch the fun," Marcus said.

The market opened limit up as had been expected, but then prices eased off the limit. The phone rang. It was Marcus's broker reporting his buy orders had all been filled. The market started moving lower. Marcus thought, *Soybeans were supposed to be limit up for three days, and they can't even hold limit up for the first morning.* He immediately called his broker, frantically giving him sell orders. Marcus was so excited that he lost count of the amount he sold and actually ended up not only getting out of his entire position, but also going significantly net short as well—short positions he ultimately bought back at much lower prices. "It was the only time I made a lot of money on an error," Marcus said.

When Marcus told me this story, it strongly reminded me of an event I had experienced during the largest bull market in cotton in the twentieth century when prices reached nearly $1.00 per pound—their highest level since the Civil War. I recall I was long cotton, and the weekly export report showed sales of a half million bales to China. It was by far the most bullish cotton export report I had ever seen. But instead of locking limit up (200 points higher) the next morning, cotton opened up only about 150 points higher and then started trading down. That opening proved to be the exact market top—a high that would not be seen again for well over 30 years.

Druckenmiller Is on the Wrong Side of the Market

In the aftermath of the fall of the Berlin Wall and German reunification, Stanley Druckenmiller held a large long position in the deutsche mark based on the premise that Germany would adhere to both an expansionary fiscal policy and a tight monetary policy—a bullish combination. He was still very heavily long at the start of the first Iraq war. Being long the deutsche mark would prove to be a very bad position in the ensuing period. Druckenmiller, however, largely avoided the impending losses, as he abandoned his long-standing bullish position in the deutsche mark, selling $3.5 billion worth in one day.

I asked Druckenmiller what caused his sudden change in opinion on the deutsche mark. He explained, "The dollar had been supported by safe-haven buying during the initial stage of the U.S. war with Iraq. One morning, there was a news story that Hussein was going to capitulate before the start of the ground war. The dollar should have sold off sharply against the deutsche mark on the news, but it declined only slightly. I smelled a rat."

The Invincible Position

In 2009, Michael Platt placed a large position in a trade that sought to benefit from a widening yield curve (i.e., long-term interest rates rising more or falling less than short-term rates). There was a succession of news items that were detrimental to the trade. Each time, Platt thought, *I am going to get screwed in this position*, and each time nothing happened. After this scenario repeated several times, Platt thought that the yield curve just couldn't get any flatter no matter what news came out. He quadrupled his position, and the yield curve went from 25 points to 210 points (albeit Platt took his profits about halfway into this move). It was his biggest winning trade of the year.

The Submerged Volleyball

Scott Ramsey is the portfolio manager for Denali Asset Management, a commodity trading advisory firm, which has an average annual compounded return of 15 percent (net) with annualized volatility of 11 percent during its 13-year history. Ramsey compared the ability of the market to shrug off a crisis event to the release of a volleyball pushed underwater. Speaking of the ability of the European and U.S. equity markets to rally to new highs a day after the European Central Bank bailed out Ireland, Ramsey said, "Think of taking a volleyball and pushing it underwater—that is your crisis event. Then you let go—the event dissipates—and the ball goes popping out of the water. That is exactly what we experienced in the markets." To Ramsey, this type of price resilience indicated that the markets were in a "risk-on" mode and very likely to continue moving higher.

Buy the Strongest, Sell the Weakest

Ramsey also believes that the relative strength of markets during a crisis can be a useful predictor. "Just a simple exercise of measuring which markets were the strongest during a crisis," he says, "can tell you which markets are likely to be the leaders when the pressure is off—the markets that will be the volleyball popping out of the water."

Just a simple exercise of measuring which markets were the strongest during a crisis can tell you which markets are likely to be the leaders when the pressure is off—the markets that will be the volleyball popping out of the water.

Scott Ramsey

Ramsey considers the relative strength of markets an important factor in all circumstances, not just crisis events. He always wants to be long the strongest market and short the weakest. As an example, when QE2 (the second phase of quantitative easing by the Federal Reserve) was ending, Ramsey expected that the shift of assets out of the dollar would stop and the dollar would recover. The question was which currency should be used as the short against the dollar. "The weak link," Ramsey said, "turned out to be the Turkish lira, which was breaking out to a two-year low against the hated dollar. If it couldn't rally versus the dollar when the Fed was printing money like crazy, what was it going to take?"

Michael Marcus made the same point about buying the strongest market and selling the weakest. "You absolutely want to put down a bet when a market acts terribly relative to everything else," he said. "When the news is wonderful and a market can't go up, then you want to be sure you are short." As an illustration, he recalled a very inflationary period in the 1970s when all the commodity markets were trading in lockstep fashion. On one particularly extreme day, almost all the commodity markets were limit up. On that same day, cotton opened limit up, but then sold off, finishing only marginally higher for the day. "That was the market peak," Marcus said. "Everything else stayed locked limit up, but cotton never saw the light of day again."

Most novice traders will seek to buy the laggards in a sector based on the premise that these markets provide the best return/risk potential because they have not yet moved as much as the others. Marcus and Ramsey are saying that traders should do the exact opposite.

Correlation as a Clue

There are periods when different markets will move in relative tandem. During such periods, the failure of a market to respond as expected to the price action of a correlated market can provide an important price clue. Ramsey cited the example of the complete breakdown in the correlation between commodity prices and equity prices in September 2011.

Following the 2008 financial crisis, previously uncorrelated markets became highly correlated, as the markets shifted between "risk-on" and "risk-off" environments. During risk-on periods, equities, commodities, and foreign currencies (versus the dollar) all tended to move higher. On risk-off days, the exact opposite price behavior prevailed.

In mid-September 2011, this correlation pattern completely broke down. Even though equity prices had rebounded to the top of a two-month trading range, copper, which is typically a leading indicator for commodity prices, was near its low for the year, completely unresponsive to the rebound in equity prices. Ramsey took this price action as a sign that commodity prices in general, and copper in particular, were vulnerable to a decline—a downtrend that subsequently occurred.

Chapter Twenty

The Value of Mistakes

❡

To do my vacuum cleaner, I built 5,127 prototypes. That means I had 5,126 failures. But as I went through those failures, I made discoveries.

James Dyson

I have not failed. I've just found 10,000 ways that won't work.

Thomas Edison

More is learned from one's errors than from one's successes.

Primo Levi

IMPROVEMENT THROUGH MISTAKES is probably a good thumbnail description of Ray Dalio's core philosophy as well. Dalio loves mistakes because he believes mistakes provide the learning experiences that lead to improvement. The idea that mistakes provide the pathway to progress permeates the corporate culture that Dalio has sought to instill in his company, Bridgewater. Dalio is almost reverential in his comments about mistakes:

> I learned that there is an incredible beauty in mistakes because embedded in each mistake is a puzzle and a gem that I could get if I solved it (i.e., a principle that I could use to reduce my mistakes in the future). I learned that each mistake was probably a reflection of something that I was (or others were) doing wrong, so if I could figure out what that was, I could learn how to be more effective. . . . While most others seem to believe that mistakes are bad things, I believe mistakes are good things because I believe that the most learning comes via making mistakes and reflecting on them.

Dalio has written down his life philosophy and management concepts in *Principles*, a 111-page document that is required reading for all Bridgewater employees. The second portion of this work is a list of 277 management rules, which, not surprisingly, includes rules that pertain to mistakes. A sampling:

- Recognize that mistakes are good if they result in learning.
- Create a culture in which it is okay to fail but unacceptable not to identify, analyze, and learn from mistakes.
- Recognize that you will certainly make mistakes and have weaknesses; so will those around you and those who work for you. What matters is how you deal with them. If you treat mistakes as learning opportunities that can yield rapid improvement if handled well, you will be excited by them.
- If you don't mind being wrong on the way to being right, you will learn a lot.

Marty Schwartz drew a contrast between trading and other careers in regard to how people respond to mistakes, "Most people, in most careers, are busy trying to cover up their mistakes. As a trader, you are forced to confront your mistakes because the numbers don't lie."

Analyzing Your Trades

Steve Clark advises traders who work for him to dissect their profit and loss (P&L) to see what is working and what is not. He says traders often don't know where their profits are coming from. Even when they do, this knowledge may be ignored. He described a common experience of traders seeking his advice who say, "I have been running this book, and these things have been going really well, but I keep losing money on this." Clark would tell them, "Do more of what works and less of what doesn't." This comment may sound like obvious advice, but it is surprising how many traders fail to follow this simple rule.

Do more of what works and less of what doesn't.

Steve Clark

The Trader's Log

Several of the Market Wizards mentioned that writing up and analyzing their trades were critical to their success. Ray Dalio traced the origin of the Bridgewater system to this process: "Beginning around 1980, I developed a discipline that whenever I put on a trade, I would write down the reasons on a pad. When I liquidated the trade, I would look at what actually happened and compare it with my reasoning and expectations when I put on the trade."

Randy McKay attributed his early success to a rigorous routine of analyzing his trades. He described beginning this process in the years when he traded on the exchange floor: "One of the things I did that worked in those early years was analyzing every single trade I made. Every day, I made copies of my cards and reviewed them at home. Every trader is going to have tons of winners and losers. You need to determine why the winners are winners and the losers are losers. Once you can figure that out, you can become more selective in your trading and avoid those trades that are more likely to be losers."

Each mistake, if recognized and acted upon, provides an opportunity for improving a trading approach. Most traders would benefit by writing down each mistake, the implied lesson, and the intended change in the trading process. Such a trading log can be periodically reviewed for reinforcement. Trading mistakes cannot be avoided, but repeating the same mistakes can be, and doing so is often the difference between success and failure.

Chapter Twenty-One

Implementation
versus Idea

~

A Post-Bubble Trade

How a trade is implemented can be more important than the trade idea itself. Colm O'Shea viewed the runaway bull market in NASDAQ in 1999 and early 2000 as a bubble. When the market broke sharply in March 2000, he was relatively sure that a major top was in place and that equities would surrender most of their prior gains. Despite this expectation, O'Shea never considered going short equities. Why? Because, as he explained, while the price rise during a bubble can be quite smooth, the price decline after a bubble bursts is typically interspersed by treacherous bear market rallies.

O'Shea thought the repercussions of a market top would be much easier to play than a direct short in equities. Specifically, he reasoned that the U.S. economy had been artificially boosted by the massive mispricing of assets. Once the NASDAQ bubble burst, O'Shea thought it was clear that the economy would slow down. A weakening economy would, in turn, lead to a decline in interest rates. So instead of implementing a short equity position, O'Shea went long bonds. Although both trends materialized—that is, stocks declined and interest rates declined—the big difference was that, as O'Shea had anticipated, the stock price decline was highly erratic, while the interest rate decline (bond price rise) was relatively smooth.

The trade was highly successful, not because the underlying premise was correct, which it was, but rather because of the way the trade was implemented.

Even though the March 2000 peak in the NASDAQ led to a plus-80 percent decline lasting two and a half years, in the summer of 2000 the NASDAQ witnessed a plus-40 percent rebound. If O'Shea had executed his idea through a short stock index position, he would have been correct in his call, but most likely would have lost money by being stopped out during this massive bear market rally. In contrast, the long bond position, which he had implemented instead of going short equities, witnessed a fairly smooth uptrend. The trade was highly successful, not because the underlying premise was correct, which it was, but rather because of the way the trade was implemented.

A Better Option

Sometimes, options may offer a much better means of implementing a trade than an outright position. Joel Greenblatt's description of his trade in Wells Fargo provides a perfect example of a situation in which an option position implied a much higher return/risk ratio than a straightforward long position.

As Joel Greenblatt explained, "In the early 1990s, Wells Fargo, which had an excellent long-term, consistent fee-generating business, came under a lot of pressure because of its high concentration of commercial real estate loans in California, at a time when California was in the midst of a deep real estate recession. It was a possibility, although unlikely, that the real estate downturn could be so severe that Wells Fargo would go through all its equity before investors could get the benefit of its long-term fee generation.

If it survived, though, the stock would likely be much higher than its current depressed price of $80, which reflected prevailing concerns.

"The way I looked at the risk/reward of the stock was that it was a binary situation: The stock would go down $80 if Wells Fargo went out of business and up $80 if it didn't. But by buying LEAPS [long-term equity anticipation securities] with more than two years until expiration instead of the stock, I could turn that 1:1 risk/reward into a 1:5 risk/reward. If the bank survived, the stock should be a double, and I would make five times my money on the options, but if it failed, I would lose only the cost of the options. I thought the odds were much better than 50–50 that the bank would survive, so the stock was a buy. But in terms of risk/reward, the options were an even better buy. The stock did end up more than doubling before the options expired."

Chapter Twenty-Two

Off the Hook

A Unique Observation

Some items of trading advice, such as the importance of risk management and the need for discipline, albeit absolutely critical, were cited by many of the traders I interviewed. Occasionally, however, a trader offered an insight that no one else had mentioned before. I particularly like these unique observations.

A perfect example of this type of trading principle was Marty Schwartz's dictum related to situations in which you are very worried about your position and the market lets you off the hook easily. Schwartz said, "If you're ever very nervous about a position overnight, and especially over a weekend, and you're able to get out at a much better price than you thought possible when the market trades, you're usually better off staying with the position."

~

If you're ever very nervous about a position overnight, and especially over a weekend, and you're able to get out at a much better price than you thought possible when the market trades, you're usually better off staying with the position.

Marty Schwartz

On the Hook

An illustration of Schwartz's observation came up in my interview with Bill Lipschutz when he described the first time in his trading career that he was truly scared. At the time, he traded a very large proprietary foreign exchange (FX) account for Salomon Brothers. It was the fall of 1988, and Lipschutz was looking for the dollar to decline vis-à-vis the deutsche mark. He explained that since the market was in a low-volatility period, his position size was much larger than normal. He was short $3 billion against the deutsche mark. It was a Friday afternoon, and Mikhail Gorbachev gave a speech at the United Nations in which he stated that the Soviet Union was going to implement troop reductions. The market took that to mean that the United States would now be more likely to cut its defense spending, which, in turn, would be beneficial for deficit reduction. In response, the dollar immediately started to strengthen.

Lipschutz fully expected the market to continue to move against him. He would have liquidated his position if he could have, but given the large size of his holdings, this action was impossible in light of the thin liquidity of the late Friday afternoon market in New York. Lipschutz thought his only possibility for exiting the position was to wait for the Tokyo open (Sunday evening New York time) when there would be much greater liquidity. In the meantime, his strategy was to keep the dollar from rallying further versus the deutsche mark in the thin Friday afternoon market. So, in an effort to push down the dollar vis-à-vis the deutsche mark, Lipschutz sold an additional $300 million. The market absorbed this large order like a sponge. There was not even a hint of weakness. Lipschutz knew he was in deep trouble.

He walked over to firm's president and said, "We have a problem."

"What is it?" the president asked.

Lipschutz replied, "I'm short the dollar, and I've misjudged my liquidity in the market. I've tried to hold the market down, but it's not going to work. And I can't buy them back."

The president calmly asked, "Where do we stand?"

"We're down somewhere between $70 and $90 million," Lipschutz answered.

"What's the plan?" he asked.

Lipschutz answered, "When Tokyo opens, I have to see where it's trading. My intention is to cover half the position at that time and go from there."

Lipschutz sweated out the weekend. Then when Tokyo opened Sunday night, the dollar was actually moving lower. The market was letting Lipschutz off the hook. Lipschutz, however, abandoned his prior plan to cover half the position in the early part of the Tokyo session. Instead, he waited. The dollar kept on sliding. Lipschutz eventually covered the entire position in the European session with an $18 million loss, which seemed like a great victory after having been down nearly five times that amount Friday afternoon.

I asked Lipschutz why he held on to his entire position when most people in his situation would have been so relieved to get out at a better price that they would have liquidated everything on the Tokyo opening. Lipschutz replied, "The reason I didn't get out on the Tokyo opening was that it was the wrong trading decision."

Schwartz Saves Me Money

I had a personal trading experience in which Schwartz's advice figured prominently. In 2011, the NASDAQ rallied sharply from a mid-June relative low into early July, approaching the highs of the entire long-term up move. The day before the release of the July unemployment report, the market set its highest close since the start of the rebound, suggesting bullish expectations for the following day's report. The actual report released the next day, however, reflected extremely bearish expectations. Typically, when an unemployment report is bearish, market commentators will find some mitigating statistic or factor. This report was so negative that commentators couldn't find any element of it that was constructive. The market sold off sharply in response to the report and continued to move lower in the ensuing hours. Then, in the early afternoon, prices began to rebound and continued to trend steadily higher for the remainder of the session. By the close, the market had erased 75 percent of the losses from the low of the day. This was a Friday, so it was also a strong weekly close, with prices finishing not far below the recent multiyear high.

At the time, I was looking for an intermediate top and had come into the day positioned extremely short. The market's ability to shrug off very bearish news, combined with a strong weekly close near multiyear highs, looked like extremely bullish price action to me. By any objective assessment of the day's price action, I had to admit to myself that I was likely on the wrong side of the market. I expected the market to open higher on Sunday night and then to see another upward leg. After Friday's price action, I was resigned to liquidating a major portion of my position beginning Sunday night and into Monday. On Sunday night, however, although I was dreading the worst, the market actually traded down 15 full points from the Friday close in the first 10 minutes. Recalling Schwartz's dictum, I liquidated only a token 10 percent of my short position. The market was much lower on Monday's equity market opening and continued sharply lower thereafter. Following Schwartz's advice had saved me a lot of money.

If the market lets you off the hook easily, don't get out.

Why does the rule about not getting out when the market lets you off the hook easily tend to work more often than not? Because—think about it—if you are really worried about a position overnight, and especially over the weekend, it will be because something dramatic has happened. Perhaps some unforeseen news has come out that is detrimental to your position. Or, perhaps, the market closed Friday with a strong breakout to new highs and you are still short. Whatever the news or development, you are hardly the only one who knows about it. On the contrary, everyone will be aware of these same facts. And if, despite developments that suggested the market should move strongly against you at the next opening, the market instead barely moves against you at all or goes the other way, it implies that there are some very strong hands positioned in the same direction you are. The lesson is: If the market lets you off the hook easily, don't get out.

Love of
the Endeavor

THE LANGUAGE THAT THE Market Wizards use to describe trading is quite revealing. Consider the following samples:

- Bruce Kovner: "Market analysis is like a tremendous multidimensional chess board. The pleasure of it is purely intellectual."
- Jim Rogers: "[The markets are] one big, three-dimensional puzzle. . . . But this puzzle is not one in which

you can spread out the pieces on a great big table and put them all together. The picture is always changing. Every day some pieces get taken away and others get thrown in."

- David Ryan: "[Trading] is like a giant treasure hunt. Somewhere in here [*he pats a weekly chart book*] there is going to be a big winner, and I am trying to find it."

- Steve Clark: "I thought I was playing a video game, and I couldn't believe I was getting paid to do it. I enjoyed it so much that I would have done it for nothing."

- Monroe Trout: "I can retire today and live very comfortably off the interest for the rest of my life. The fact is that I like to trade. When I was a kid, I loved to play games. Now I get to play a very fun game, and I'm paid handsomely for it. I can honestly say that there isn't anything else I would rather be doing. The minute I don't have fun trading, or I don't think I can make a profit, I'm going to quit."

What do all these quotes have in common? They are all gamelike analogies. This tells you that for the Market Wizards trading is not a matter of work or a matter of getting rich. Rather, trading is something they love to do—an endeavor pursued for the fun of the challenge.

It is not a matter of work. It is not a matter of getting rich. Rather, trading is something they love to do—an endeavor pursued for the fun of the challenge.

When I interviewed Bill Lipschutz, I was struck by how trading permeated his life. One physical manifestation of this complete integration of trading into his daily life was the presence of quote monitors in every room, including one next to his bed so that could roll over, half asleep, to check prices. He even had a monitor at standing height in the bathroom—a self-mocking statement of his obsession with the markets, or a manifestation of it, or perhaps both.

I asked Lipschutz, "With trading consuming most of your day, not to mention night, is it still fun?"

"It's tremendous fun!!" he answered. "It's fascinating as hell because it's different every day. . . . I would do this for free. I'm thirty-six years old, and I almost feel like I have never worked. I sometimes can't believe I'm making all this money by essentially playing an elaborate game."

There we go, another game analogy. Interviewing the Market Wizards, it becomes clear that they are drawn to trading because they love the challenge of winning what in their eyes is a complex game. They are trading because they love trading. They are not trading to achieve some other goal, such as getting rich, and that makes all the difference.

Responding to my question of what determines who will succeed as a trader, Colm O'Shea said, "Frankly, if you don't love it, there are much better things to do with your life. . . . No one who trades for the money is going to be any good. If successful traders were only motivated by the money, they would just stop after five years and enjoy the material things. They don't. . . . Jack Nicklaus had plenty of money. Why did he keep playing golf well into his sixties? Probably because he really liked playing golf."

I am sure that if you look at the people you know who are successful, regardless of their occupation, you will find that the one thing they have in common is that they love what they are doing. It is true for trading. It is true for any pursuit. Love of trading may not guarantee success, but its absence will likely lead to failure.

Appendix

Options—Understanding the Basics[1]

T HERE ARE TWO BASIC types of options: calls and puts. The purchase of a call option provides the buyer with the right—but not the obligation—to purchase the underlying item at a specified price, called the strike or exercise price, at any time up to and including the expiration date. A put option provides the buyer with the right—but not the obligation—to sell the underlying item at the strike price at any time prior to expiration. (Note, therefore, that buying a put is a bearish trade, while selling a put is a bullish trade.) The price of an option is called a premium. As an example of an option, an IBM April 210 call gives the purchaser the right to buy 100 shares of IBM at $210 per share at any time during the life of the option.

The buyer of a call seeks to profit from an anticipated price rise by locking in a specified purchase price. The call buyer's maximum possible loss will be equal to the dollar amount of the premium paid for the option. This maximum loss would occur on an option held until expiration if the strike price was above the prevailing market price. For example, if IBM was trading at $205 when the 210 option expired, the option would expire worthless. If at expiration the price of the underlying market was above the strike price, the option would have some value and would hence be exercised. However, if the difference between the market price and the strike price was less than the premium paid for the option, the net result of the trade would still be a loss. In order for a call buyer to realize a net profit, the difference between the market price and the strike price would have to exceed the premium paid when the call was purchased (after adjusting for commission cost). The higher the market price, the greater the resulting profit.

The buyer of a put seeks to profit from an anticipated price decline by locking in a sales price. Like the call buyer, the put buyer's maximum possible loss is limited to the dollar amount of the premium paid for the option. In the case of a put held until expiration, the trade would show a net profit if the strike price exceeded the market price by an amount greater than the premium of the put at purchase (after adjusting for commission cost).

Whereas the buyer of a call or put has limited risk and unlimited potential gain, the reverse is true for the seller. The option seller (often called the writer) receives the dollar value of the premium in return for undertaking the obligation to assume an opposite position at the strike price if an option is exercised. For example, if a call is exercised, the seller must assume a short position in the underlying market at the strike price (since by exercising the call, the buyer assumes a long position at that price).

The seller of a call seeks to profit from an anticipated sideways to modestly declining market. In such a situation, the premium earned by selling a call provides the most attractive trading opportunity. However, a trader expecting a large price decline would usually be better off going short the underlying market or buying a put—trades with open-ended profit potential. In a similar fashion, the seller of a put seeks to profit from an anticipated sideways to modestly rising market.

Some novices have trouble understanding why a trader would not always prefer the buy side of the option (call or put, depending on market opinion), since such a trade has unlimited potential and limited risk. Such confusion reflects the failure to take probability into account. Although the option seller's theoretical risk is unlimited, the price levels that have the greatest probability of occurrence (i.e., prices in the vicinity of the market price when the option trade occurs) would result in a net gain to the option seller. Roughly speaking, the option buyer accepts a large probability of a small loss (cost of the premium) in return for a small probability of a large gain, whereas the option seller accepts a small probability of a large loss in exchange for a large probability of a small gain (premium income).

The option premium consists of two components: intrinsic value plus time value. The intrinsic value of a call option is the amount by which the current market price is above the strike price. (The intrinsic value of a put option is the amount by which the current market price is below the strike price.) In effect, the intrinsic value is that part of the premium that could be realized if the option were exercised at the current market price. The intrinsic value serves as a floor price for an option. Why? Because if the premium were less than the intrinsic value, a trader could buy and exercise the option and immediately offset the resulting market position, thereby realizing a net gain (assuming that the trader covers at least transaction costs).

Options that have intrinsic value (i.e., calls with strike prices below the market price and puts with strike prices above the market price) are said to be in-the-money. Options that have no intrinsic value are called out-of-the-money options. Options with a strike price closest to the market price are called at-the-money options.

An out-of-the-money option, which by definition has an intrinsic value equal to zero, will still have some value because of the possibility that the market price will move beyond the strike price prior to the expiration date. An in-the-money option will have a value greater than the intrinsic value because, if priced at the intrinsic value, a position in the option would always be preferred to a position in the underlying market. Why? Because both the option and the market position would then gain equally in the event of a favorable price movement, but the option's maximum loss would be limited. The portion of the premium that exceeds the intrinsic value is called the time value.

The three most important factors that influence an option's time value are:

1. *Relationship between the strike price and market price.* Deeply out-of-the-money options will have little time value since it is unlikely that the market price will move to the strike price—or beyond—prior to expiration. Deeply in-the-money options have little time value because these options offer positions very similar to the underlying market—both will gain

and lose equivalent amounts for all but an extremely adverse price move. In other words, for a deeply in-the-money option, the fact that risk is limited is not worth very much, because the strike price is so far from the prevailing market price.

2. *Time remaining until expiration.* The more time remaining until expiration, the greater the value of the option. This is true because a longer life span increases the probability of the intrinsic value increasing by any specified amount prior to expiration.

3. *Volatility.* Time value will vary directly with the estimated volatility (a measure of the degree of price variability) of the underlying market for the remaining life span of the option. This relationship is a result of the fact that greater volatility raises the probability of the intrinsic value increasing by any specified amount prior to expiration. In other words, the greater the volatility, the greater the probable price range of the market.

Although volatility is an extremely important factor in the determination of option premium values, it should be stressed that the future volatility of a market is never precisely known until after the fact. (In contrast, the time remaining until expiration and the relationship between the current market price and the strike price can be exactly specified at any juncture.) Thus, volatility must always be estimated on the basis of historical volatility data. The future volatility estimate implied by market prices (i.e., option premiums), which may be higher or lower than the historical volatility, is called the implied volatility.

On average, there is a tendency for the implied volatility of options to be higher than the subsequent realized volatility of the market until the options' expiration. In other words, options tend to be priced a little high. The extra premium is necessary to induce option sellers to take the open-ended risk of providing price insurance to option buyers. This situation is entirely analogous to home insurance premiums being priced at levels that provide a profit margin to insurance companies—otherwise, they would have no incentive to assume the open-ended risk.

Notes

― ≈ ―

Chapter One: Failure Is Not Predictive

1. www.baseball-almanac.com/feats/feats23.shtml.
2. In many futures markets, the maximum daily price change is restricted by a specified limit. *Limit down* refers to a decline of this magnitude, while *limit up* refers to the equivalent gain. If, as in this case, the equilibrium price that would result from the interaction of free market forces lies below the limit-down price, then the market will *lock* limit down—that is, trading will virtually cease. Reason: There will be an abundance of sellers, but virtually no willing buyers at the constrained limit-down price.

Chapter Four: The Need for an Edge

1. The question presupposed that you were going to play roulette, which ruled out the even better strategy of not playing at all.

Chapter Five: The Importance of Hard Work

1. There is some controversy on the cause of Bender's death, as the Costa Rican authorities charged his wife with murder. Knowing his wife and speaking to a close friend of Bender familiar with the details, I am inclined to believe the suicide version of the story.

Chapter Eight: Risk Management

1. Readers unfamiliar with options can skip this section or first read the Appendix before returning to this section.
2. Performance statistics obtained from www.barclayhedge.com.
3. Multiple former employees of SAC Capital either pleaded guilty or were convicted of insider trader. The firm itself also pleaded guilty to insider trading charges, paying a total of $1.8 billion in fines. Steve Cohen was charged with failure to properly supervise employees, but not with directly participating in insider trading. Nevertheless, the aforementioned convictions and the fact that Cohen routinely encouraged managers who worked for him to share their trading ideas have led to controversy over whether, and to what extent, Cohen's trades may have benefited from insider information. As far as I see it, you could cut Cohen's returns in half and still have an exceptional track record. Whatever the influence of insider trading on Cohen's record (if any), it was certainly much smaller than this amount, or else there certainly would have been more than enough evidence for Cohen to have been charged directly. Thus, from a purely statistical perspective, I still believe there is little question that Cohen is a highly skilled trader. These comments are only intended to explain why I believe Cohen is a great trader, regardless of what assumptions might be made about the influence of insider trading, and in no way are intended to imply that he directly participated in insider

trading—I am unwilling to speculate on this matter—or to condone such action if he did.

Chapter Nine: Discipline

1. Many futures markets have limits on the maximum price move that is allowed to occur on any single day. If an event causes a great imbalance between buyers and sellers, as was the case after the announcement of the Carter plan, futures will move to the limit price with virtually no trading occurring. Futures will continue to experience limit price gaps on successive days until the market finally reaches a level where there are enough balancing orders for the market to trade freely—in this instance, until the price had fallen far enough for buyers to enter the market.

Chapter Twelve: Losing Is Part of the Game

1. Portions of this section have been adapted from Jack D. Schwager, *Market Wizards*, new ed. (Hoboken, NJ: John Wiley & Sons, 2012).

Chapter Fifteen: Size Matters

1. The strategy was rebranded as the Omni Global Fund in February 2007. Prior to that time, the strategy was called the Hartford Growth Fund and was not open to outside investors.

Chapter Sixteen: Doing the Uncomfortable Thing

1. Daniel Kahneman and Amos Tversky, "Prospect Theory: An Analysis of Decision under Risk," *Econometrica* 47, no. 2 (March 1979): 263–291. Prospect theory is a branch of decision theory that attempts to explain why individuals make decisions that deviate from

rational decision making by examining how the expected outcomes of alternative choices are perceived (definition source: www.qfinance .com).

2. This paragraph has been adapted from Jack D. Schwager, *Market Sense and Nonsense* (Hoboken, NJ: John Wiley & Sons, 2012).

Chapter Seventeen

1. Treasury bill prices move inversely to Treasury bill interest rates.

Appendix: Options—Understanding the Basics

1. This appendix was originally published in *Market Wizards* (1989).

About the Author

~

Mr. Schwager is a recognized industry expert in futures and hedge funds and the author of a number of widely acclaimed financial books. He is currently a principal of PortfolioFit (portfoliofitadvisors.com), an advisory firm that specializes in constructing tailor-made futures and FX managed account portfolios for clients, and the co-portfolio manager for the ADM Investor Services Diversified Strategies Fund, a portfolio of futures and FX managed accounts. Mr. Schwager is also one of the founders of Fund Seeder (Fundseeder.com), a platform designed to find undiscovered trading talent worldwide and connect unknown successful traders with sources of investment capital.

Mr. Schwager is the inventor of the Jack Schwager Commodity Index (JSCI) family, a set of dynamically adjusted commodity indexes that incorporate spread structure, systematic inputs, and voalitlity-based risk adjustments. The indexes are scheduled to be launched in early 2014 in cooperation with Aquantum AG and UBS.

Previously, Mr. Schwager was a partner in the Fortune Group, a London-based hedge fund advisory firm. His previous experience also includes 22 years as Director of Futures research for some of Wall Street's leading firms.

Mr. Schwager has written extensively on the futures industry and great traders in all financial markets. He is perhaps best known for his best-selling series of interviews with the greatest hedge fund managers of the last three decades: *Market Wizards* (1989), *The New Market Wizards* (1992), *Stock Market Wizards* (2001), and *Hedge Fund Market Wizards* (2012). His latest book *Market Sense and Nonsense*, a compendium of investment misconceptions, was published in November 2012. Mr. Schwager's first book, *A Complete Guide to the Futures Markets* (1984) is considered to be one of the classic reference works in the field. He later revised and expanded this original work into the three-volume series, *Schwager on Futures*, consisting of *Fundamental Analysis* (1995), *Technical Analysis* (1996), and *Managed Trading* (1996). He is also the author of *Getting Started in Technical Analysis* (1999), part of John Wiley's popular *Getting Started* series.

Mr. Schwager is a frequent seminar speaker and has lectured on a range of analytical topics including the characteristics of great traders, investment fallacies, hedge fund portfolios, managed accounts, technical analysis, and trading system evaluation. He holds a BA in Economics from Brooklyn College (1970) and an MA in Economics from Brown University (1971).